C0-DAL-470

Shining the Light on All the Right

Celebrating the Art of Nursing Around the World

Mark and Bonnie Barnes
Co-founders of The DAISY Foundation

with Jim Eber

Published by The DAISY Foundation™
Cover Design: Romana Bovan
Interior Design: Eliot House Productions
© 2024 Mark and Bonnie Barnes. All rights reserved.

This publication is designed to provide accurate and authoritative information in regard to the subject matter covered. Reproduction or translation of any part of this work beyond that permitted by Section 107 or 108 of the 1976 United States Copyright Act without permission of the copyright owner is unlawful. Request for permission or further information should be addressed to The DAISY Foundation™.

Library of Congress (LC) Cataloging-in-Publication Data
Names: Barnes, Mark, author | Barnes, Bonnie, author | Eber, Jim, Author (with)
Title: Shining the Light on All the Right: Celebrating the Art of Nursing Around the World
Description: Trade paperback second edition | Anacortes, WA: The DAISY Foundation™, 2024
Identifiers: LCCN 2024908328 | ISBN 979-8-990-36290-1 (softcover)
LC record available at https://lccn.loc.gov/2024908328

Printed in the United States of America

The DAISY Award® is a registered trademark and the property of The DAISY Foundation™.

To Patrick, whose spirit lifts DAISY

The DAISY Story

An End & A Beginning

"Patrick is in the hospital.".......................................3

Now What Do We Do?
1999–2008

Liquid Dinner 19

Picking the First DAISY 25

Getting It 37

The Healer's Touch... 49

A Broken Promise 59

The Power of Stories and Gratitude 71

Funding Our Future 87

Growing DAISY
2008–2019

I Like You 99

We Are Family 109

What Happened to Turnkey?! 119

Shining a New Light 133

All We Wanted to Do Was Say Thank You 147

Nursing Our Future
2020–2024

Fire. 163

A World of Gratitude 169

We Are a Bigger Family 183

Nursing the Power of Recognition. 191

Shining the Light on People Who Have Helped Make DAISY Right

Twenty-Five Years of Gratitude 203

Index. 229

An End &
A Beginning

"Patrick is in the hospital."

That's how the message from Tena started: "Patrick is in the hospital." But he's going to be fine, she said. No need to call. No need to come home from Italy. Enjoy your vacation. We just wanted you to know.

Of course Pat will be fine. He and Tena had welcomed their first child, our first granddaughter, Riley, six weeks earlier. When we saw them after she

3

was born, Pat was more than fine; he was over the moon for Riley. So were we. *Of course Pat will be fine.*

We called anyway.

Tena took us through what had happened. Pat had been pretty tired a few nights before. He turned down dessert, which he never did, and went to bed early. In the middle of the night, he woke up and said, "Something's wrong." He had blood blisters in his mouth and petechiae or small red dots on his arms, stomach, and legs. They thought it looked an allergic reaction, but to what? Whatever it was, it was not normal. They needed to get him to an emergency room. Thankfully, some family was visiting, and they took Pat to Baptist Saint Anthony Medical Center while Tena stayed home with the baby.

At first, the doctors also thought it was an allergic reaction, perhaps to one of the medications Pat took, though none of them had caused any problems before. They took him off his meds and monitored him closely but 24 hours later he wasn't getting better. Meanwhile a blood test had revealed an extremely low platelet count, hence the blood blisters and red dots, as platelets help the blood clot normally. His doctor admitted him to the hospital under the care of the hematologist while they worked on a diagnosis.

There were several possibilities for what was happening, from aplastic anemia to leukemia, and they ran tests for all of them. As Tena listed the possible causes, we were concerned but not panicked, because the doctors had no test results yet and Tena sounded calm. Besides, Pat was resilient. He had already beaten Hodgkin's disease—twice—as an adult. His first diagnosis was during his senior year in college. He still graduated despite missing half the fourth quarter. The second time he beat Hodgkin's, he was 26, not long before he met Tena. He had also recovered just fine from his hip replacement the year before. We—like Tena—resolved to stay positive until there was a reason not to be positive.

Turns out, it wasn't leukemia. Or aplastic anemia. The diagnosis, made almost by process of elimination, was idiopathic thrombocytopenic purpura or ITP. We had never heard of ITP, and neither had Tena, and this being 1999, it wasn't like we could pick up our smartphones and ask Google. Tena had learned all she could from Pat's doctors and what she could find with her Mac and a dial-up modem. None of what she heard or read sounded too scary. The doctors had described ITP as Pat's immune system being "disorganized" and destroying his platelets. No one knows why some people get it or what causes it, they explained, but it affects both children and adults. In children, it usually goes away without treatment or they grow out of it in time. In adults, it's more serious but still treatable. It also can become a chronic condition, so Tena and Pat would need to monitor him after he was treated and sent home.

But Pat wasn't being sent home. ITP usually clears in adults with the first course of treatment: The immune system is suppressed with a course of prednisone to reboot and reorganize it. If the prednisone doesn't work, a second alternate course of treatment typically does. The prednisone didn't work. They were starting the second treatment when Tena sent us the message. But she still didn't want us to worry.

"I'm not worried," Tena said on the phone. "You don't need to come home." We came home.

❋ ❋ ❋

Tena felt a little guilty cutting our vacation short. What if by the time we got there the second treatment worked and Pat was fine and ready to go home? But he wasn't and she was glad we were there. The family staying with Pat and her had to leave, and they had no one else in Texas who could stay with the baby. With Pat in the ICU with an immune disorder, there was no way she could bring a six-week-old baby with her. She felt alone and grateful for the company, help, and someone to calm her nerves as they treated Our Patrick.

That's what we called him, "Our Patrick." That's what everyone who loved him called him. Patrick was Mark's son from his first marriage. He was an adult when Bonnie met him, yet she felt that connection to him soon after they met. She felt an even deeper connection to Mark, who had been a business associate of hers years before they started dating. In 1996, she retired from a high-level career in advertising in Los Angeles and New York City, moved to Sonoma, and married Mark. With no connections to the region, she spent her days volunteering and learning to grow and tend grapes, converting a few acres from an untamed dog run into a vineyard while Mark continued running his advertising business in San Francisco.

Pat and Tena had ended up in Amarillo because of his job. He started his career in advertising sales working for Mark's company in Los Angeles and then moved to the Atlanta office where he met Tena, who also worked for Mark. Actually, Pat and Tena worked together, and she remembers her first impression of him: "He was a bit of a jerk." Luckily, Pat got a second chance to make a first impression, and it didn't take long for Tena to discover Our Patrick: a funny and fun-loving guy who, having beaten cancer twice, felt lucky to be alive. Mark often says that Pat was a natural salesman. His knowledge of his field and easy way with people served him and his clients well. This extended to his chemotherapy for his second bout with Hodgkin's: He would walk around the unit with his IV pole and visit with other patients, giving them encouragement, telling them it was going to be okay. Pat was a guy who knew no strangers and whose warmth, humor, and outgoing nature made people feel comfortable. He lived each day with gratitude and joy—except when someone cut him off while driving. We knew where Riley would learn her first curse words.

Tena and Pat married in 1994. Soon after, they moved to Memphis where Pat had been offered a job. Then he was offered his first job as a manager in Amarillo. *Amarillo?* Neither he nor we nor anyone in either family had ever been to Amarillo, but we knew the owner of the company offering Pat the job. So when he asked Pat and Tena to visit the city and meet the people in the office, we offered to meet them in Amarillo.

Any one-light-dirt-road-tumbleweed ideas we had about Amarillo were wrong. While Mark and Pat headed to the office, Bonnie drove around with Tena and found a modern city with a great shopping mall, a golf club, movie theaters, a bowling alley, and neighborhoods of lovely homes for Pat and Tena to raise their family in.

Any ideas we had that by the time we got there Patrick would be laid out by something as enigmatic as ITP were similarly wrong. When we made it back to Amarillo from our vacation in Italy, Pat was running his business from his bed. He was so pumped up on prednisone and other medications, he was talking a mile a minute. Make that two miles. Pat usually talked a mile a minute. Looking at him, we initially figured we'd be there for a few days and be back home soon. "I'd give anything to be able to change a diaper," he joked. Our Patrick really seemed to be fine.

Once again, we were wrong. Our Patrick was not fine.

* * *

By the time we arrived in Amarillo, the second course of treatment hadn't worked, and we moved in with Tena and the baby, living out of our vacation suitcases. A friend picked up our car at the San Francisco airport. Mark's father was living with us at the time, and he took care of our dogs. Our neighbors watched over them all while we watched over Pat and tried to make sense of his bizarre condition and what the doctors told us.

A third treatment failed. The doctors moved to the next. The nurses counseled us to have patience. Have faith. Let the next treatment do its job. Keep Patrick's spirits high. Not that Pat was having any trouble with that. The nurses weren't going to let whatever this ITP thing was get him down, and neither was he. He engaged each and every one he came in touch with, and they got to know him. When one of his night nurses, Dan, discovered Pat loved sports and that his recall for facts was voluminous, he sat up with Pat on nights he couldn't sleep sparring sports facts, taking his meals with him, and staying late. Mornings after Dan had been up with him, Pat couldn't wait to tell us how he had bested Dan on some arcane sports question.

What Pat was having trouble with was food. A mouth full of blood blisters made eating difficult, and he had very little appetite. Each day we tried to entice him with a different treat he loved. Nothing interested him until the day Mark brought a Cinnabon cinnamon roll to Pat's room for his own breakfast. Pat smelled it and asked for a bite. He proceeded to eat the entire thing and asked us to bring him another the next day. "Be sure to bring enough for all the nurses in the unit too as a thank-you," he said. So we did. And that afternoon, Pat got moved into a VIP room down the hall. Ignoring all rules about correlation and causation, we concluded either they needed Pat's closet-sized room for something more important or that bringing nurses Cinnabon results in being moved to a bigger room with a sofa and big TV. We like to think it was the power of Cinnabon and Patrick. Well, it made sense at the time.

But what Cinnabon and nothing nor anyone had the power to do was make Pat better. The fourth course of treatment failed. As did the fifth, sixth, and seventh courses. They gave him platelet transfusions. Nothing moved the proverbial platelet needle. As Pat worsened, he started to bleed into his lungs and bladder. He struggled to hide the pain and stay positive, as did we.

The doctors began to question if they had the correct diagnosis. They reran all the tests to see if they missed something. They did bone marrow aspirations to make sure his body could still manufacture platelets. It could, but as soon as it did, it attacked and destroyed them. The hospital consulted James George, a physician and ITP specialist from Oklahoma City, who recommended another course of action: a bone marrow transplant. The Amarillo hematologist concurred. "All the signs point to ITP," the doctors told us. "We don't understand why he's not responding. It may be something bigger is going on. A bone marrow transplant would enable him to stop making more antibodies than platelets and start to reverse the course of his condition." The only problem was Baptist St. Anthony's Medical Center didn't do bone marrow transplants, so the doctors recommended two options: MD Anderson Cancer Center at the University of Texas or Fred Hutchinson Cancer Research Center in Seattle.

The choice was an easy one for us: We all wanted to go to Seattle. Fred Hutch had pioneered bone marrow transplants, but more importantly, Patrick was born and raised in the city. His sister was still there and a good enough genetic match for the transplant. His brothers Brad and Adam were also there. So was our dear friend Dianne, who offered her home to all of us, including Tena's mother, one of Tena's friends, and Pat and Tena's beloved golden retriever, Griffey—named for Pat's favorite baseball player on his favorite team: Ken Griffey Jr. of the Seattle Mariners.

The hospital made the arrangements to get Pat to Seattle on an ambulance plane. And for the first time in weeks, instead of worrying, Pat and Tena felt optimistic. "We were actually excited," Tena remembers. "This is it! This is the fix. We know it's a long road, but this is what's going to make him better." We all got swept up in the news and sprang into action. Bonnie said, "I'll fly with him." Mark said he would help Tena pack up the house and get her on the plane with the baby and the dog and then drive Tena's car with all their stuff from Texas to Washington. We were ready to relocate to Seattle for as long as it took to get Pat well.

There was something else to celebrate that day, too: Pat and Tena's fifth anniversary. We thought it would be lovely if we took care of Riley so they could have dinner together. The nurses loved the idea. They found out what his favorite restaurant was and ordered his favored dish: spaghetti dinner. They decorated his room and set everything up. We bought some pearls for Pat to give Tena, picked up dinner, and delivered it all.

Pat and Tena toasted with their water glasses.

"You're going to get better," she said.

"I'm going to get better."

* * *

On the plane to Seattle, it was just Patrick, Bonnie, the pilot, and Robert, a nurse from Amarillo. Pat was struggling from the pain and a serious nosebleed, but Robert was unfazed and managed it all in the tiny space with words and limited resources. Robert's priority was keeping Pat comfortable, ensuring that his pain didn't reach a crisis level—which was a real risk as Pat's internal bleeding worsened on the plane—but through it all he also noticed Bonnie's fear and dread and found the time to be compassionate with her. It was at that moment in her mind the nurses went from being "Pat's nurses" to "our nurses."

And our nurses had all they could handle when Pat was admitted to Fred Hutch. His internal bleeding had grown dangerous. He hallucinated that a woman was screaming she needed help and he ripped out his tubes and ran down the hall to save her. By the second night, the bleeding in his lungs had become a real problem. He was having trouble breathing. The doctors called us in the middle of the night to inform us that Pat needed to be put on a ventilator and would need to be put in an induced coma. The three of us got to the hospital at 4:00 A.M.

Before Pat was sedated, he wrote us a note. Five words: *Please don't leave me alone.*

We made sure we kept that promise. We told our nurses about Pat's request, and they were incredibly respectful of it and of us. In fact, they made us part of Patrick's team. No one was ever asked to leave the room when any clinician came in, although we did volunteer to leave during certain procedures. We took the night shift, coming into the hospital at around 7:00 P.M. and leaving as soon as the day shift arrived at 9:00 A.M. or so. The rest of the family and friends shared the daytime. Tena came every moment she could while we helped with the baby at home.

Soon after Pat was intubated, our doctor called a family meeting. He knew the recommendation was that he get a bone marrow transplant, but he told us frankly he wasn't sure Patrick could survive one in his state. He was weak. His body could not fight infection, nor clot blood. The doctor, however, still believed it was ITP and wanted to continue to treat for that, starting an eighth course of treatment for him. The nurses brought in all kinds of new equipment—pumps, monitors, machines. They were totally adept at using and explaining each one to us. ("Okay, this test that we're doing, this is what we're hoping for. This is when we should see some results.") Our nurses warned us not to panic when an alarm sounded on one of the machines. It didn't necessarily mean that Pat was in distress, and they promised to respond quickly to identify the issue. We watched as they studied Pat. They had an expectation of what was right and what was less right, not from looking at the monitors but by watching him. Their judgment was remarkable, and we all were struck by the smallest changes they picked up on and how quickly they responded to them.

The nurses' care for Patrick went beyond the patient and focused on the person. We were moved by the way our nurses touched him. There was a tenderness, a gentleness, an affection for Pat. They asked us to bring in a photo of him, and taped it to the entrance of his room. That way, whenever anyone came in, they were reminded of the vital, healthy, handsome man, son, husband, friend, and new father who was in their care, not the intubated prednisone-swollen man in the induced coma attached to all those tubes and monitors. They asked us what Pat cared about, what he liked to do, what he did for a living. One of our nurses told us that despite the coma he was in, he might well be able to hear us. This nurse shared an experience he had when his father had been sedated after open heart surgery and woke up to recount a family conversation that had taken place at his bedside while he was unconscious. After the nurse told us this story, we stayed positive and upbeat when we were in Pat's room, and everyone heeded our request not to mention in front of Pat that the Seattle Mariners had traded Ken Griffey Jr. to the Cincinnati Reds.

But while our nurses were always focused on Pat, they also focused on us. The doctors were amazing, but they were not always there, and when they were it was sometimes hard to understand and process all they told us. It seemed we always had questions after they left the room or hung up the phone. *What about this? What exactly does that mean? Why did you say that? What happens if . . . ?* We relied on our nurses to answer all these questions and more, fill us in, and explain things in layman's terms. They never made us feel we were asking stupid questions, even though we suspected we were. Nor did they get annoyed if we asked the same question more than once, which we know we did. A lot.

The more nurses educated and involved us, the less helpless we felt, but as with Pat, the nurses went beyond the clinical to get to know us, too. They made sure we were eating and getting some sleep during the day. They asked what Riley was doing as they looked at her pictures that covered Pat's room. They made sure they got to know Tena too, even though she was home most of the time taking care of Riley, who could not visit her dad and be exposed to any kind of infection. The closest Riley got to him was before we left Amarillo. Tena drove alongside the hospital, and our nurses got Pat to the window where Tena held Riley up so he could see her. It was a bit of a metaphor for Tena's whole situation: feeling painfully torn between

Pat and Riley, always feeling on the outside. So we put a sign on the wall of Pat's room so she would never be or feel left out by anyone: TENA'S IN CHARGE.

We learned just how much our nurses knew about us during the night that Pat first involuntarily extubated his ventilator. Given the amount of blood in his lungs, it went flying everywhere as the tube came out. It was the most upsetting thing we had ever seen or experienced. Our nurse that night was Tana, a seasoned, confident clinician who no doubt had been through this kind of thing hundreds of times. Nothing was too dramatic, scary, or critical to throw her. At least that's how it seemed to us when we screamed our heads off calling for her. She appeared instantly and took control of the situation. She knew Mark has a hard time seeing blood, so she threw him out of the room so he wouldn't faint. Then she put Bonnie to work, knowing that she would need to help in some way—to *do something*. In no time, Tana had the ventilator back in place, Bonnie had helped clean Patrick up, and Mark was back in the room and breathing.

Tana left to awaken the resident to report what had happened, while we just sat there completely shaken. When she returned to the room, she came right over to Bonnie and wrapped her arms around her. Then she did the same to Mark. If we didn't know it before, then we sure knew it then: Nurses give the best hugs. And we would need every one of them and more over the next weeks.

Sometimes the hugs were literal, sometimes figurative. One morning, a nurse named Karen saw Bonnie in the hallway waiting for Mark so they could leave after a rough night. She looked at Bonnie: Ghostly remains of yesterday's makeup covered her face, her eyes red and bleary. She asked Bonnie if she would be seeing Tena when we got home. "Yes," Bonnie answered, "she will no doubt be up with Riley." Karen nodded. "Bonnie, I hate to say this to you but if you go home to Tena looking like you're looking? She's gonna think he died. You just can't do that. I need you to go into the bathroom and wash your face. Please put some makeup on. Put some lipstick on. Put in your contact lenses. I don't want Tena to see you this way." Then she gave Bonnie a real hug.

Bonnie couldn't believe Karen had the guts to say that to her, but she was glad she did. It was kind, thoughtful, and empathetic—not for Bonnie but for Tena, a person whom Karen barely knew, only that she was in charge.

Not that there was anything Tena or any of us could do but be by Patrick's side—stay and pray. We all knew what we had known since Amarillo: You can only live so long without platelets to defend against infection or internal bleeding, and Patrick had no platelets. Even sedated, he was still declining. Every day, another issue: low blood pressure, low-grade temperature, concerns about infection, coughing, low oxygen saturation, bleeding in his stomach that required a tube to drain . . . it didn't matter how great the hospital or doctors were. Whether they had the latest technology. Whether they were the most attentive clinicians in the world. Whether they gave him transfusions by the gallon. It was a horrible, sad, frustrating, worrisome, anxious time for all of us. Every day we hoped against hope to walk in and find his platelets had gone up and they would wake him up. Every day we learned a little more about how gruesome ITP can be. One day, Pat started bleeding into his eyes, which meant that when he woke up, he likely would be blind. Yet we kept saying *when*, not *if*. *When* they turn Pat's immune system around, are there going to be other complications that we needed to think about? What did we need to prepare for? Tena was a realist. She didn't want to get caught up in "he's going to get better and everything's going to go back to the way it was." Our Patrick was still alive but would be disabled. She and Bonnie started making a plan for living with those disabilities while caring for a baby. Which, for a brief shining moment nearly a month after Pat arrived in Seattle, seemed to be soon.

A lab report revealed the antibodies in Pat's blood that were destroying his platelets were dropping. He had been getting plasma pheresis, the removal and exchange of blood plasma, and there seemed to be results in platelet production—they appeared to be coming back. "We are seeing a light here," his doctor said. He was "cautiously optimistic." Knowing we hadn't been home in more than two months, Tena told us to go home and do our laundry, get stuff we needed, check in with Mark's dad and the dogs, and come back in a couple of days. We agreed and flew back to Sonoma. We made it home by midnight, hugged Mark's father and the dogs, and crashed.

At 3:00 A.M., the phone rang. It was Tena. "You had better come back," she said. The moist blood in Pat's lungs had created a problem. If it was an infection, they could treat it. If it was a mold, there was nothing they could do to stop it. He would die. By the time we made it back to Fred Hutch, they knew. It was a mold.

We had hours until the end. Family and friends said their goodbyes first. Then Tena. And Riley. As the door shut behind them, we stood on either side of Patrick and held his hands. A nurse whose name we don't know, but whose face and touch we will never forget, held our hands in hers. Another nurse came in to turn off the ventilator. It didn't take long.

On the early afternoon of November 6, 1999, eight weeks from the time he was first admitted into the hospital in Amarillo, J. Patrick Barnes passed away in Seattle.

Only then did we leave him alone.

❀ ❀ ❀

The days after were filled with feelings of loss and love—and occasional laughter. While planning the celebration of his life at the country club he used to go to as a kid, we went with Tena to a funeral home that gave a 50 percent discount to anyone who died at Fred Hutch. Pat was going to be cremated but he apparently still needed to be in a box. We walked through the displays with names like Eternal Slumber and Whispering Pines with price tags of $25,000, $50,000, and more. Then we found it: The Cardboard, $200. We all had the same reaction: Pat would love it. He always loved a deal.

After the celebration, we headed back to Amarillo with Dianne to get Tena, Riley, and Griffey settled and to plan another celebration of Patrick's life for their friends and colleagues there. Our thoughts also turned to keeping Patrick's spirit alive after the celebrations of a life taken too soon were over. Pat had been gone for a week and left a gaping hole in our world we felt compelled to fill. And so the emptiness that consumed us was joined by a question—a question countless people ask in some way every day. A question that for us would define the work we would do for the rest of our lives.

Now what do we do?

J. Patrick Barnes and his daughter, Riley, August 1999

Now What Do We Do?

1999–2008

"The DAISY Foundation allows me to live out my mission of inspiring nurses to be the best they can be by putting a spotlight on excellent nursing care and having a platform for nurses to see what a great nurse looks like."

Jennifer Magill, BSN, RN

Liquid Dinner

A father should get to know his newborn daughter. That baby girl should get to grow up with her devoted dad. A couple that has found true love should get to grow old together. Parents shouldn't lose a child—ever. That's not the way the world is supposed to work. But it happens. People leave us too soon. More than they ever should. More than anyone can or could prevent or understand. We lost Our Patrick: our son, husband, and father. When going through a loss this deep, it's only natural to feel the need to do something—*anything*—to fill the void.

On our second night in Amarillo, with the loss still raw and deep, we decided to fill that void with a liquid dinner: a lot of wine and a lot of tears. We headed to Outback Steakhouse with Tena and Dianne. And with Riley swinging in her baby swing on the side of the table, we came back to the question: *Now what do we do?* What were we going to do in Patrick's memory?

As the wine and tears flowed, we came up with three ideas. The first idea was the most obvious for a family struck down by a disease that they had no hope of understanding and could not be stopped: prevent what happened to Patrick from happening to someone else, so no patient and family would ever go through what we went through. We would start a nonprofit in Patrick's memory. We would fund research to cure ITP. We would call it The Foundation for the Elimination of Diseases Attacking the Immune System. Tena thought about the name. *Too long*, she thought, turning it over in her head. She then suggested shortening it and creating an acronym: **D**iseases **A**ttacking the **I**mmune **SY**stem or DAISY. The DAISY Foundation—in Memory of J. Patrick Barnes. Perfect.

The second idea originated with Bonnie: provide support for patients going through what Patrick went through who had no family to be by their side every day. She remembered how we were often the only family at the Fred Hutch bone marrow unit. There were patients in rooms up and down the halls, but they were usually alone. This was long before the days of sitters and Skype, and it had upset her and Mark. She wanted to find a way for people to not be alone in a place like Fred Hutch, where patients come from all over the world for treatment and don't have people to do what we did. Our foundation would coordinate volunteers to be with people when they were sick, to provide emotional support. So that, extending Patrick's final words to them, they did not have to be alone.

Up until this point, our liquid dinner ideas had been entirely too sad. We had a collective desire to focus on something positive, on something good because so much bad had happened. Besides, Pat was such a positive person. He would hate if everything a foundation set up in his memory did focused on what was wrong and did not celebrate all the right. As we thought about this, we kept coming back to our nurses. We fixated on them. We all talked about how we expected the clinical excellence, particularly at Fred Hutch, but we did not expect the way it was delivered and how the nurses made us feel. We remembered how important it was to the nurses caring for Patrick that they get to know him, even the ones he never spent a conscious minute with. They treated Pat like a whole person—who he was before he got sick and the man he would be once again when he was well. Tena said she would never forget how kind, gentle, loving, and tender they were, yet always professional and informative. They were her lifelines. They were her family before we returned to Amarillo from Italy.

We recalled stories of our nurses from the last two months. Dan and his sports trivia. The welcome delivery of Cinnabons that seemingly made us VIPs. The spaghetti dinner on their fifth anniversary. Tana making sure Mark did not faint on the floor when Pat involuntarily extubated his ventilator and blood flew around the room. Karen making sure Bonnie did not go home looking like Pat had died. The picture of Pat taped to his door. Every time nurses touched Patrick with loving hands. Every time they took the time to speak with us as we sat by his bedside in the middle of the night. Every hug.

The only sad part of our nurse conversation was realizing there are far too many Patricks in the world. As unique as it might feel to us and to every other person out there who is losing someone, especially someone too young to die, our situation was not unique. Nurses have seen just about everything, from the routine to the unimaginable. But *we* felt unique, and our nurses treated us this way. Maybe they had seen it all and saw everything as part of their job, but for families like ours and patients like Patrick, they saw us as individual human beings in their care. We then realized nurses are not always doing this in the service of making a bad or sad situation more bearable. Many times, it's a joyful time: helping a family welcome a child, making pain go away, treating someone sick and watching them get better. Every day, millions of nurses do one little thing to make patients feel like our nurses made us feel: that the patients are more than just charts and numbers in the system. That the patients are human beings, and so are the people who love them.

Our nurses comforted us and gave us the comfort level to feel it was okay to go get a cup of coffee, take a shower, get some sleep. They made our last days with Patrick more bearable. Less horrible. More human. They were, like Tena said, an extension of our family, and lifelines to the doctors and information we needed. We couldn't have trusted them more. After all, we trusted them with Patrick's life. How many people felt just the way we did and wished there was a way to thank them? How many nurses don't even see how what they do is so extraordinary, who just see it all as doing their job? They are unsung heroes to so many.

The more we talked, the more we truly felt Patrick's spirit guiding us at the table, reminding us how the nurses took care of him, leading us further into this idea: doing something to thank our nurses who had been so great to us and are so great to others around the country. And thanks to Tena we even had a name for it all: the DAISY Award—like the flower, reflecting the beauty and joy we wanted our work to embody, its roots in our mission of gratitude and Patrick's story. The DAISY Award would be a recognition program for nurses to honor and celebrate them all year long, sharing their stories of extraordinary compassionate care. We would start by sharing our story and honoring nurses at the two hospitals that took care of Pat and then grow from there. We would make sure the award wasn't a competition and that it was more than just an appreciation program or employee-of-the-month kind of thing. We wanted the DAISY Award to be something nurses were nominated for by other nurses—something that came from the heart and recognized moments of compassionate care like our nurses had given us. Our premise was: Who knows nurses better than other nurses? Knowing how busy nurses and hospitals often are, we resolved to make the whole process and ceremony turnkey; we would provide everything they needed to get going and to implement the program on an ongoing basis, so they could easily honor nurses all year long. We would also make it flexible so the hospitals could customize the program to fit their needs and cultures.

We could feel the energy of Pat's memory running through us as we moved on to what we might give the nurses who received the recognition. A certificate. A pin, of course—nurses love pins. Did you see all those pins they wore? Bonnie thought that since they work so hard and never think of themselves, we should give them a dinner for two at a nice restaurant and a massage so they could get back some of the physical comfort that they gave to their patients. We resolved to open a bank account as soon as we got back to California and start funding all three DAISY ideas ourselves while we applied for nonprofit status from the IRS. We would help cure ITP, support families, and recognize nurses. We would execute all of them immediately. Or so we thought.

DAISY HONOREE STORY[*]

Rebecca Schmit, BSN, RN
Children's Hospital Colorado
Aurora, Colorado

Becca has done so much with our Palliative Care Team in the NICU. I worked on day shift caring for one of my primary patients who was on palliative care while Becca was caring for him on night shift. She suggested the idea of a "bucket list" for our patient and his siblings, parents, and extended family members to check off while he was with us.

The family came up with ideas and Becca was the ringleader in getting the items on the list checked off. She was so creative with her ideas on how to pull off some of the activities! One of the things on the list was to have a day at the beach. Becca brought in play sand, a blow-up kiddie pool, a beach ball, sand toys, and even managed to borrow a heat lamp from the OR to make the "sunshine!" The family was elated and his siblings so enjoyed playing with him while he dipped his feet in the sand and water while wearing his swim trunks basking in the "sun" on night shift.

Becca arranged to have a Disco Dance Party, which was also on the bucket list. She brought in a plastic ball and some rhinestones so that his sisters could decorate the disco ball and get in on the fun as well. Another item on the list was to have a Nerd Day, and Becca made a onesie painted to look like it was a button-up oxford shirt with a pocket protector and some pencils inside. She found baby-size black glasses and put tape around the bridge of the nose. The pictures were so adorable!

The family would always be in such high spirits when Becca was around. She helped so much more than she realized! Not only did she inspire the patient's family, but she also inspired those of us who are privileged to work with her. She showed me that with just the right amount of heart and creativity, anything you can dream up is possible to do, even while in a Neonatal Intensive Care Unit!

I think it is very clear that Becca is a true DAISY Nurse. She would never expect such recognition for what she sees as just a part of her everyday life on the job.

_____

* All DAISY Honoree stories in this book are reprinted as submitted by the nominator, edited only for privacy, small grammatical changes, and length. These stories are just a tiny fraction of the DAISY nominations we've received. Many more can be found on our website.

> *"We don't do this work for the recognition or thanks, but it was such an amazing feeling to receive the DAISY Award! It's so gratifying to be appreciated by those you care for and the team that helps you every day."*
>
> Angela Bacon, BSN, RN, CCRN

Picking the First DAISY

I n the fairy tale movie about the making of the DAISY Foundation, we meet the doctors who can cure ITP soon after our liquid dinner and present them with all the money they need to make it happen. No one ever suffers from an immune disorder alone in a hospital. The DAISY Award rolls out with ease in Patrick's two hospitals, followed in hospitals across the nation clamoring to recognize and thank the unsung nurse heroes. Also, in that movie, Mark is played by British actor Idris Elba, and Bonnie plays herself. But reality is often a lot more work and not quite as pretty.

Things started well enough. We returned to Sonoma after Pat's memorials and funded a DAISY bank account. We filed the paperwork for 501(c)(3) nonprofit status with the IRS (which would be granted the following spring). A few business associates of Mark's made significant donations in Pat's memory and smaller amounts came in from family, friends, and others. By the end of 1999, we had about $50,000 in contributions in addition to our own, plenty to start our DAISY work.

Of course we also had our own work. Mark was back running his business in San Francisco. Bonnie was back running the vineyard and serving on the board of the grape growers association, doing their marketing and strategic planning. And Tena and Riley were with us. We had become very close to Tena during Pat's final journey. We had Thanksgiving in Amarillo, and then Tena returned to Sonoma with us. She had been building an advertising career in Atlanta and Memphis, but in Amarillo she had been an administrative assistant. There was no career for her to build there, no support network, and without Pat, no reason to stay. She needed to get back into advertising and make enough money to support herself and Riley. As much as we wanted them to stay in Sonoma and let us help with Riley, the cost of living was so high in California we couldn't afford to buy her a house, and the commute to San Francisco was so far she would never have time with Riley. It wasn't going to work. Instead, Tena's parents, who had moved away from Atlanta, said if she moved back there they would move back too, and help take care of the baby when she went to work. We promised to visit regularly.

So it was down to us and Dianne, who was back in Seattle, to move on with DAISY. DAISY just didn't want to get moving that quickly.

Our first idea that we could fund research to cure ITP started out well: We supported the work of Dr. George in Oklahoma City, who had consulted with Pat's doctors in Amarillo and recommended the bone marrow transplant. He and his students were researching treatment protocols for ITP. In a related idea, we decided to support the treatment of ITP by encouraging people to register as bone marrow donors and to help run blood drives. (The first one being held in Amarillo with the help of Pat's former employer and friends.) But the following year our idea that we could fund research to cure ITP faded as quickly as you could say $200,000. That's what the doctor who took us out for a nice dinner told us. We ended up giving him $25,000 to partially pay for a data analyst, and regretted it almost instantly. Another doctor who had developed one of the drugs that was tried on Patrick but did not work met with us and said it would cost $100,000 just to open a door to a research facility. We backed out of his door politely instead of making the same mistake.

Our second idea that we could create a national support network for patients alone in hospitals fizzled after we sobered up and thought things through. We realized it was probably impractical to develop and tend to a network of volunteers. We didn't know enough people to even lay the groundwork at the hospitals we knew, and there was no control over when people would be needed. But while we abandoned our idea for creating a support network on our own, we planned to help the ITP Support Association in the United Kingdom and the Platelet Disorder Support Association in the United States, both of which served patients with diseases like the one Patrick had. We hoped they could establish a network of compassionate and caring people to reach out to families affected by immune system disease.

Our first two ideas from the liquid dinner might have been on a bumpy path, but we did present them upfront in our first official announcement of the DAISY Foundation "dedicated to Pat's memory, positive spirit, and sense of humor." The nurse recognition program that would define DAISY for the next two decades was in the announcement, too. We talked about how fortunate we were to have had the support of such competent and compassionate doctors and nurses. How touched we were by their dedication and grace. How the nurses in particular were our unsung heroes. How we were thus establishing a recognition program for nurses who provide extraordinary compassionate care featuring a personalized thank-you, dinner at a wonderful restaurant, and a spa treatment. And if that sounds exactly like where we were months before, then give yourself a DAISY pin. Actually, the DAISY pin was one of the few parts of the DAISY Award we were able to move forward on. We created it and the DAISY Award certificate. We just had no one to give them to . . . yet.

We started out hopeful. We decided to take our idea for the DAISY Award program to Fred Hutchinson Cancer Research Center in Seattle first. We flew back to Seattle to present it and got a positive reaction from the managers of Patrick's unit but also some news: Implementing it immediately would be impossible. Fred Hutch, which had been renting inpatient space at Swedish Hospital, had joined with the University of Washington Medical Center and Seattle Children's to create the Seattle Cancer Care Alliance. The new alliance would be housed at the university and planned to open its first inpatient unit in 2000. If we wanted to wait a year or so, they would be happy to revisit our idea.

We decided to wait. We felt we couldn't go to the other hospitals until we knew it worked in the place that last took care of Patrick—the one that shared our story. While we waited, we revisited our idea. We still had confidence in it. We even enhanced it, adding the delivery of Cinnabons for all the nurses on the unit, just like Pat had asked us to do in Amarillo—just like he would have done himself if he had survived. But then we started thinking: Those rolls had gone over big time with his nurses, but would DAISY? We knew from our research there was no national nursing recognition program for compassionate care. But maybe there was a reason for that. How were the nurses going to respond? Was this going to cause conflict? Even if it wasn't a competition and was given on a regular basis, would it be perceived as a competition? We come from advertising. We have been through award seasons and heard the polite applause when people win and then heard the chatter that they didn't deserve it. We didn't think nurses would be like that, but what did we know? The Cinnabons would make sure that they celebrated together but could they prevent conflict and jealousy? Would they eat them and still walk away mad? *Would DAISY's desire to shine a light on the positive be seen as a negative?* We would have our answer soon enough.

We also wondered if any of Patrick's nurses remained at Fred Hutchinson. Without them to honor, we didn't think anyone there would connect to Pat's and our story and DAISY as deeply. We were wrong. Turned out, two people at the UW Medical Center felt that connection: Cindy Angiulo and Susan Grant. Two people who would mean more to the foundation's future than we ever could have imagined when we met them and learned our first DAISY lesson in the power of great relationships.

❋ ❋ ❋

There's an old saying that there are always three sides to every story: yours, mine, and the truth. In thousands of presentations about DAISY's origin, we have told the story of how from the start we wanted the nurses' recognition to be based on a nomination from their colleagues for their compassionate care, not clinical excellence. No manager or administrators playing favorites or playing office politics. No names picked at random from a hat. Yet picked from a hat is exactly how the Seattle Cancer Care Alliance at UW Medical Center decided to proceed with their first DAISY Award in February 2001.

Our story has always been that it really upset us, and it did, because a few of Patrick's nurses did remain at Fred Hutch and could have been honored through a nomination by a fellow nurse. What we have never shared is that we knew the recipient would be chosen at random. We supported that approach at first, because if we hadn't, we knew DAISY might never have been awarded at all.

It was a letter from Dianne on DAISY's behalf dated November 20, 2000, written following her conversation with a university hospital administrator we have no recollection of meeting, that revealed this truth to us. Most of it covered the basics about rewarding one nurse per month with a dinner and spa treatment and presenting the award and pin along with a delivery of Cinnabons to the staff. It talked about Pat and our desire to keep the program as simple as possible, as well as flexible: "their opinions and desires would determine our next course of action." And then there was this: "Here's how the program might work. You determine the recipient of the month randomly as we discussed."

Shining the Light on All the Right

It was nearly two decades after Dianne wrote this letter that we found it in an old file and read it again. Both of us wondered *Why would we have agreed to that?* Not Dianne, *us.* We spoke with one voice when it came to DAISY. There was also a line about keeping the value of the dinner and treatment under a certain dollar amount. Why? Because Dianne knew much more than her letter stated. She knew what the university wanted and needed in order for Cindy Angiulo to launch the program—and we would be forever grateful for that. Because Cindy was our first guardian angel.

When we had met Cindy earlier in the year, she captured our hearts as much as she says we captured hers. Cindy was the assistant administrator nurse at UW Medical Center at the time and had made it her charge to put the DAISY program together there to support her work with the Seattle Cancer Care Alliance. Just before Pat passed away, Cindy had been tasked with building a new nursing culture at the university around the Alliance. She not only had to bring the nurses from the other organizations together as university employees but also had to recruit new nurses and get them all working together for something different from what she or any nurse had experienced. On top of that, everybody including the university's nurses had to rebid for their positions, from the top down. "It was a very stressful time," Cindy recalls. "Nobody knew what the new environment would be like. Even after the first ten beds opened it was a shaky time culturally for everything there. People were used to what they were used to."

DAISY, Cindy thought, was something different, too. She felt integrating DAISY would fit into what she was trying to accomplish. She had decided to implement it regularly into the weekly offsite education day for all the nurses. "It was very special. It added to the good feelings nurses had in having a day devoted to them. It was something everyone could agree on and support. My whole goal was integrating nurses from three different organizations. DAISY could unify everyone. There was nothing better that we could do. But we had to be thoughtful as to the politics of it." That's because DAISY wasn't for all the nurses in the medical center, only for the Seattle Cancer Care Alliance, and that created some controversy. The Fred Hutch unit was a showcase for the university, but she had to be careful that didn't scream their nurses were better than any others at the university's medical center. And it being a state institution, Cindy had to be cautious about what they gave as gifts. Hence the dollar limit.

Then there was controversy around selecting the recipients, which explained the rest of Dianne's letter. Cindy hated the idea of the random drawing as much as we did. She wanted specific criteria for nominations or at least to get nurses' nominations together and then put *them* in the theoretical hat, not *every* nurse's name. But she had not been involved in those discussions. The university saw the idea of the drawing as inclusive, nonthreatening, and easier. Cindy didn't agree with the first point, but she saw the value in the other two. "It was a very tenuous time," she recalls. "Folks were threatened by much more than just DAISY in this new environment, and leadership didn't want anyone to feel more threatened. They wanted DAISY implemented, but they wanted to avoid any dissent. A drawing meant they didn't have to agree on anything. They just had to pick a name."

In the end, they picked two—Kenna Smith Shangrove and Carolyn Stormer—and we travelled to Seattle in February 2001 to present with Dianne the DAISY Award for the first time. We brought the award certificates, the frames for which Mark had spared no expense at Costco. We brought the pins. We brought the Cinnabons. We brought more family who wanted to share in a day that honored Patrick. As we walked from the car into the building, we felt great anticipation: What would we experience? What would the nurses be like? *What would we say?*

It seems silly to us now—given that DAISY today has a sample script with very specific instructions on what presenters are to say and how to make it truly mean something to the nurses—that we would have prepared nothing. But that story is the truth. We didn't know what DAISY would become, and the first recipients were not chosen as we imagined. So we winged it. We talked about what a great experience we had being with them, that they were kicking us off, what DAISY meant to us, a bit about Patrick and his care, and how we just wanted to say thank you. We presented them with the pin and certificate, which they loved, and gift certificates for dinner for two and a massage that

Bonnie had arranged at two local places. The university honored the nurses they had chosen and said they would carry on with the program. We urged them to do it every month and make it an experience the honorees would remember for the rest of their lives.

What we were also unprepared for was how fast these nurses dashed any of our fears that there would be tension or unintended negative consequences as a result of getting a DAISY Award. Kenna and Carolyn were terrific. The other nurses all said things like "You couldn't have picked better nurses" and "This is great." We could only think how great it would feel if the nurses themselves nominated the recipients, which is exactly what Cindy Angiulo arranged to do next.

As the Alliance's unit got bigger and the team evolved together, their reputation at the university soared. That changed everything, so Cindy moved to make the changes she and we wanted: coming up with objective criteria for the nominating process and allowing nurses to do the nominating. She saw in DAISY the possibilities for creating more

Presenting the first DAISY Award to Kenna Smith Shangrove at the University of Washington Medical Center, Seattle, February 2001

than a great culture: She also pushed to expand it beyond the one unit to all three floors of the new Alliance and even to ambulatory care. She knew that stories of great nurses were everywhere: "I love stories that celebrate inspiring others to be the best they can be and recognize people. It's always been about the stories. DAISY captured the intimacy of the care *all* nurses provide. We're given a gift to be in the lives of patients and families and there's no more intimate time ever."

There was just one problem: They didn't get any nominations from nurses. That's when we learned another important lesson about nurses that is true to this day: They don't see themselves as heroes. It's just who they are and what they do. If we had a nickel for the number of times nurses who received a DAISY said, "I'm just doing my job. I'm not doing anything special," we'd have thousands of dollars more to spend on DAISY. So after two months, we asked if the university would open it up to patients. Bonnie made up patient nomination forms and marketing materials to show them how it could work. Cindy loved the idea. But to do that she needed help advocating for the change. She needed the buy-in of the university's chief nursing officer, Susan Grant, who couldn't have been more on board.

※ ※ ※

We had met Susan in March 2000, not long after she started at UW Medical Center. She came from the Dana Farber Cancer Institute in Boston where she had spent significant time implementing programs that involved patients and families. She was moved by the idea of DAISY being that kind of program.

"When I met Bonnie and Mark, I was overwhelmed," she remembers. "Here was a family whose son had passed away and they wanted to recognize nurses and the impact that the nurses had on his care. They were representing not only their own voices but wanted to represent the voices of other patients and families. Really recognizing nurses and being able to define and highlight what outstanding and excellent nursing care looked like from the patient and family standpoint. For nurses, there's nothing more meaningful than to be recognized by patients and/or their families and to know that you've done something that made a difference for them. I knew in my core this was profoundly valuable."

Susan also knew there was no better place to pioneer this than the University of Washington. After all, it was the first hospital ever to receive Magnet designation through the Magnet Recognition Program® of the American Nurses Credentialing Center, demonstrating its excellence in nursing and patient outcomes. Being a Magnet hospital meant the university excelled in recruitment and retention of registered nurses. It was a place where nursing and professional practice were already valued. DAISY was a natural fit.

In addition, Susan didn't think DAISY would or should stop at the Alliance or the university, either. She believed there wasn't a chief nursing officer in the country who wouldn't want the DAISY program in their organization. It would give family members and patients an avenue to express how great their nurses were and how compassionate their care had been. She vowed to help make that happen.

And she did—and she was mostly right about all of what she thought. But as we said, reality isn't as pretty and takes much more time. Time that tested our resilience.

DAISY HONOREE STORY

Intensive Care Unit Team
Southern New Hampshire Medical Center ICU
Nashua, New Hampshire

There was a patient being cared for in the ICU for a month with end-stage pulmonary issues. He initially made progress but then began a steady decline and was unable to tolerate minimal life activities without intense shortness of breath. The ICU team spent a lot of time with the patient and family helping them choose a plan of care. The patient chose to not be resuscitated and ultimately wanted to remove his oxygen all together and be made comfortable. The ICU staff developed a significant bond with this patient and family and admired their strength and courage. The patient wanted to spend one last weekend with his family on his own terms. The ICU and Respiratory staff made every effort to compassionately honor his end of life requests.

While the ICU team was waiting for this patient's family to arrive from out of state, they had time to talk with him about his life and his family. It was clear how much he adored his family, and he mentioned that he had some young grandchildren. One nurse was trying to think of ways to make the experience less upsetting for his family when they arrived, so she asked more about them. The patient told her that he had a tradition of eating Oreos with his grandkids every time they visited at home, but instead of just giving them the Oreos, he would hide packages of them all around the house like an Easter egg hunt. His tradition with his own children was that they would drink a little scotch together every now and then. He and his wife also owned horses.

The nurse made a trip to the retail pharmacy across the street from the hospital and bought a bunch of Oreos, mugs for the scotch, and two little unicorns for him to give to his wife as a last present, because she couldn't find horses. She hid the Oreos all around the room while he was sleeping so that he would be surprised when he woke up. The respiratory therapist went to pediatrics to scout out decorating supplies, and she and the rest of the nurses helped to cut out paper hearts to decorate the room while the patient was sleeping.

When he woke up, he was so excited that there was a surprise that he could share with each member of his family. The nurse, leading this effort, was able to watch the grandchildren do the Oreo hunt in the patient's room. Pediatrics also gave the ICU a light-up wand, which the patient thought was just the best thing. He had so much fun showing it to his grandkids. When the family first arrived, everyone looked so anxious. The nurse escorted the family into the room to an experience that was fun instead of scary, and the grandchildren got to do something that was familiar to them. These activities provided a great deal of comfort for his wife.

"This little pin can mean so much. It keeps nurses going. Pushing, fighting, striving to be better. To do more. Recognition from the people we care for is the steam in our engines."

Megan Mowatt, BSN, RN

Getting It

Bonnie: "We had a fight."

Mark: "It wasn't a fight."

Bonnie: "It felt like a fight to me."

Mark: "It was an aggressive discussion with loud voices."

Bonnie: ". . ."

❀ ❀ ❀

We're remembering an afternoon in July 2004, more than three years after we presented our first awards at the University of Washington Medical Center. Twenty hospitals had signed up for the DAISY Awards. We had celebrated hundreds of nurses. But adding those hospitals, sustaining them, and making sure the nurses availed themselves of the spa treatment and dinner was proving difficult and time consuming. An entrepreneur by trade and at heart, Mark saw the hours Bonnie was putting into DAISY—the cold calling, the hurry-up-and-wait, the follow-up—and he was frustrated. Not unhappy, frustrated.

"What the heck are we doing here?" Mark aggressively wondered. "Every hospital is just as hard as the last one. You're working very hard for very little. The amount of time spent calling and calling. The constant questioning. All to give this to people and places who don't seem to want it. Something's not clicking. Maybe we should just focus on sustaining what we have."

Bonnie understood where Mark was coming from. They were both proud of how far DAISY had come but its growth was not proportional to Bonnie's effort. Results seemed to be flagging: We were on pace to add fewer hospitals than the year before. "I was making cold calls and people were turning us down. It was free, patient- and family-generated, turnkey. Still, I would hear, 'Is this for real?' They were skeptical 'You want to do what? At no cost?' Many more of those responses than 'How do we start!?'" Bonnie also heard a refrain that would follow DAISY for the first years of its journey: Nurses didn't need recognition for the things they do every day.

Yet Bonnie remained optimistic—not "cautiously optimistic," words she and Mark swore never to use again after hearing them from the doctor the day before Patrick died, but fully optimistic. Hence, the fight . . . um, aggressive discussion. After all, DAISY had come so far—which was exactly why Bonnie didn't share Mark's frustration. The DAISY Awards *were* growing, more than we had expected when we presented our first awards in 2001. The University of Washington *Daily* covered that event, and Bonnie told them we hoped we would get to say thank you to nurses in ten hospitals around the country. We had doubled that. Twenty hospitals might be less than one-half of 1 percent of all the hospitals in the United States, but it was an accomplishment, especially for something that had never been done before, led by people who weren't from the healthcare industry. Things were happening. DAISY had donors and sponsors. We had attended presentations at every new hospital and seen what it meant to the nurses. Some of those hospitals had had no connection to us in the beginning, which had not been the case when we launched DAISY.

＊ ＊ ＊

Actually, the first DAISY hospitals had come fairly quickly after UW Medical Center and Baptist Saint Anthony in Amarillo, where Pat's final journey began, and they came largely from relationships we or the people we knew had with those hospitals. Cedars-Sinai Medical Center in Los Angeles was the third to join and came through Lynne Doll, a dear friend of ours from the advertising world who later joined our board (and whom we sadly lost to cancer in 2010 at the age of 48). After her father died at Cedars-Sinai, Lynne told Bonnie he had received great care, and Bonnie asked if he had any great nurses. "We had incredible nurses," Lynne replied. Bonnie suggested we bring DAISY to the hospital, and Lynne and her family loved the idea of honoring her dad's nurses with the DAISY program. Lynne offered to sponsor it as a tribute to her father. Lynne's doctor was a world leader in brain surgery, and when his nurse became the hospital's first honoree, he came over to us and thanked us after the presentation. "This is really special," he said.

Sonoma Valley Hospital, where Mark's father passed, came soon after Cedars-Sinai. His homecare nurse, Steve Turme, received their first award. We added a hospital in Reno when the daughter-in-law of close friends of ours, Judy and Bruce England, gave birth to twins very prematurely. When one of the babies died, the England family helped us bring DAISY to Washoe Medical Center (which became Renown Health). Santa Rosa Memorial Hospital started after good friends got into a car accident and were treated there. All in all, we had seven hospitals presenting DAISY Awards by the end of 2002, including the first from a cold call: NewYork-Presbyterian Weill Cornell Medical Center in New York City.

Bonnie, a born and bred New Yorker, wanted to do something—*anything*—to support the city she loved after the 9/11 terrorist attacks and thought the DAISY Award would do some good. She chose NewYork-Presbyterian because of its world-renowned burn unit. She thought victims of the attack must have been taken there. She waited several weeks to reach out because she figured the hospital must be overwhelmed. When she felt it was appropriate to call, Bonnie realized she didn't know whom to call. She still didn't fully understand the structure of nursing. She tried the general volunteer line and nursing offices first and got no response. When Bonnie finally got someone to call her back and explained what DAISY wanted to do, the person knew exactly whom to put us in touch with: the director of nursing operations, Cynthia Godfrey. She listened to the DAISY story and why Bonnie had reached out to them in particular. She told Bonnie she was partially right: The burn unit had indeed been overwhelmed immediately following the attack with some of the most severely burned and badly injured patients they had ever seen. Every resource the hospital could spare shifted to the burn unit. The entire hospital had been prepared for the halls to be lined with beds, but had not received nearly as many victims as expected. Many escaped, but few still in the World Trade Center towers at the time of their collapse survived. But if Bonnie still wanted to bring DAISY to NewYork-Presbyterian in general, she said she would support it.

As we did for every hospital in our first years, we flew in to present the first award. Presenting in New York City was a tremendous experience—almost as tremendous as the sports jacket the first honoree had to wear. The nurse was a lovely Irish man, John Fiddler, who was big on compassion but small in stature. After a wonderful ceremony, Cynthia arranged for a lunch with the hospital's chief operating officer, Richard D'Aquila. He took us and the nurse to the Faculty Club (something he would do for future DAISY Honorees while he was in that position). Only problem: Jackets were required. As the award and the lunch were a surprise, John hadn't worn a jacket to work. The club had a spare on hand, but the size 48 swam on his much smaller frame.

⁂

While that nurse had no hope of filling out that jacket, DAISY was filling out quite nicely, it seemed, and we wanted to make sure everyone knew. We had started a newsletter in December 2000, announcing the launch of DAISY. It featured our first logo: a bunch of supermarket daisies we photographed in Dianne's kitchen in Seattle. The July 2001 newsletter announced our first three hospitals. In November 2002, the newsletter proudly listed the names of 76 DAISY recipients. Around this time, we also launched our first website. Looking back, we can't believe how rudimentary it all feels, yet wholly and genuinely reflective of DAISY at the time: homemade, grassroots, and of course fully honoring Patrick's memory.

In those early newsletters, we also announced proudly that we had received a grant from Johnson & Johnson, which was starting their campaign for nurses. Yes, it took us more than a day to fill out what felt like a 5,000-page application. But while it was a lot of work for the $1,000 we received, it was our first external affirmation of DAISY from a major company that had never met us, and it was a meaningful amount of money to us at the time. We received the same grant and a little more in the following two years but, then Johnson & Johnson dropped their grant program. As much work as it was for applicants to fill out an application, the company realized it was more work to read all of them!

We also announced our first corporate sponsor for a specific participating organization in our early newsletters: America West Airlines (which later became USAir), the company that helped us develop our entire approach to corporate sponsorship.

We met America West through one of our early partners, Hospice of the Valley in Phoenix. We had been introduced to the Hospice by a friend of Bonnie's mom. The Hospice was headed by Susan Goldwater Levine, the widow of the former senator and presidential candidate, Barry Goldwater. She is also a nurse—the kind of nurse who would jump out of a moving car to save someone. We know this because she almost did jump out of our moving car when we saw an accident. A motorcycle had been hit by a car. Susan tended to the motorcyclist, holding him, giving him a moment of comfort before he died. It was a very disturbing thing for us to experience—a man dying in Susan's arms like that—but it showed us who she was and is: a nurse through and through.

That evening, we attended the Hospice of the Valley fundraiser as her guests. We had a table and a DAISY sign prominently displayed, explaining DAISY's mission. America West was there, too. Their head of government affairs was impressed with what we were doing. He had lost his wife at the Hospice, and the nurses there had made a huge difference to him. We asked if he might like to sponsor the DAISY Award at the Hospice as a way of saying thank you to those nurses. He agreed, and that led to our connection to the airline sponsoring DAISY in hospitals in their most active destinations, such as Charlotte and Pittsburgh. Over the years, America West staff would join us at DAISY Award presentations—something we learned would be an important offer to future industry partners, such as Hill-Rom, a manufacturer of healthcare equipment. We were introduced to Melissa Fitzpatrick, then Hill-Rom's chief clinical officer, a nurse who loved what we were doing and saw the potential for a mutually beneficial relationship. We felt strongly from the start that we didn't want to depend on "checkbook charity." We wanted to partner with companies that shared our passion for nurses and with which we would develop unique marketing relationships. Hill-Rom became our model for that.

And then there was Cinnabon. Its cinnamon rolls were one of the happiest memories we had of Patrick during his final months, and we wanted them to be a part of every DAISY presentation. So we reached out. We started appropriately with the marketing director to ask the company to donate or at least sell us Cinnabons at cost. He refused our call. But unlike at NewYork-Presbyterian, we knew exactly where to go next—to the person who's really in charge of most companies: the boss's secretary. Within minutes of explaining DAISY, we got a call back from the same marketing director who earlier had refused our call. He agreed to pay for a box of Cinnabons for every box we bought. Soon after, a box full of thousands of $5 gift certificates arrived in the mail. When those ran out, Cinnabon sent more. We sent the hospitals personal checks to cover the other half.

Years later, Cinnabon got a new president, Geoff Hill, and public relations director, Jennifer Dempsey. Jennifer saw the meaning in what we were doing for nurses, and how DAISY might benefit the Cinnabon brand. So she invited us to come to Atlanta to meet Geoff. Over dinner, after hearing us describe DAISY and how we had integrated Cinnabon into every DAISY Award presentation, he said, "We're not doing nearly enough for you. What more can we do?" Mark told him that we were writing personal checks to hospitals to pay for half the Cinnabons they bought. Geoff said, "Well, that's going to stop. We'll pay for them all." But as each bakery was a franchise, Geoff asked that we make a presentation to his Franchise Advisory Council to get final approval. The presentation went great, and we asked Jennifer to join our board. As DAISY grew, we added hospitals in areas where Cinnabon didn't have bakeries. Jennifer's solution was to provide jars of its signature Makara cinnamon. We called it "DAISY Dust." Just like the cinnamon rolls, it served as a sweet reminder to nurses that they make a difference in patients' lives. Cinnabon continued to donate rolls nationally until we outgrew their franchise system and we had to discontinue the program in an official capacity, which wasn't easy for any of us. (Most hospitals accepted it, but there was one that threatened to discontinue the program without the free Cinnabons. They didn't.) To this day, however, the company supports DAISY with a National Nurses Week giveaway of Cinnabons to nurses and provides them at DAISY conference events. They have donated more than one million of their cinnamon rolls.

But perhaps no relationship in those nascent years meant more to DAISY's growth than Bonnie Lasky.

❀ ❀ ❀

Bonnie Lasky is a long-time friend of ours, and by 2001 she had retired as the risk manager at the University of California at San Francisco and San Francisco General Hospital. The Bonnies had been close during the time Patrick was hospitalized. Knowing Bonnie Lasky's experience, over lunch one day Bonnie said, "Come and work with us on the DAISY program."

Bonnie Lasky jumped right in. She saw we only had a few hospitals and little way for others to find out about DAISY without hearing from us. So she got her stepdaughter, Rebecca, to help create that first website. After the website was up and running, Bonnie Lasky said, "Let's go to all the UC [University of California] hospitals." She had been the assistant director at UC Davis Medical Center in Sacramento before she went to San Francisco, and she introduced us to the chief nursing officer, Carol Robinson. DAISY did the work from there. "I know nurses are doing great things every day in this hospital," Carol told us. "DAISY will give us a way to capture their stories and celebrate them." Bonnie Lasky also opened the door at other hospitals that she knew, like Children's Hospital Oakland and the Alta Bates Hospital also in Oakland. But perhaps as much as the introductions, Bonnie gave us insight. She told us, "Every hospital has its own personality and way of doing business." For example, San Francisco General had to go through the city council, which had a lot of rules and regulations on what the hospital could do. Understanding that got us ready to deal with county and safety net hospitals—where nurses really deserved to be recognized but it would take some time to get through the system.

Bonnie Lasky's influence was our first big education in the power of relationships within the hospital world to open doors, and why we knew it would take a lot of patience, persistence, and resilience to get DAISY growing. It was bound to move slower than Mark the entrepreneur wanted. Our process of forming those relationships and developing them, and our learning from and listening to nurses, was just beginning. We were new. It was bound to be messy. We needed to help nurses and hospital administrators get it—to see why DAISY and its ongoing recognition of those nurses was important—and then we needed to be patient when things dragged a bit. Still, by mid 2003 we had five new DAISY hospitals thanks to Bonnie Lasky, and we asked her to be the first nonfamily member to join our board to help us through it all.

But even with all Bonnie Lasky's help, we couldn't open all the doors we needed and wanted to. Our momentum seemed to be slowing as we entered 2004. Which brings us back to our "aggressive discussion" that summer. Bonnie understood Mark's frustration with DAISY's growth and, despite her optimism, didn't want to torture him more than necessary. So she made a promise: "Just let me get to 50, and I'll quit. Let me get 50 hospitals, and I'll stop cold calling and just run what we have." Mark agreed, and Bonnie became more determined than ever to get those hospitals and honor those nurses with the recognition and the spa treatment and night out they deserved. Well, all except the spa treatment and night out. They went away in the following year because of one woman: Ann Dechairo-Marino, the chief nursing officer at one of our DAISY hospitals, Northridge Medical Center in Southern California.

Bonnie knew in her head that Mark was right about the amount of energy she was putting in to get the spas and restaurants lined up for nurses who mostly didn't take advantage of them. But Bonnie couldn't let it go. She feared taking these gifts away from nurses, especially those in hospitals where DAISY was already established, would make future honorees feel they were worth less than the ones who came before. It was Ann who changed her mind. We were at Northridge Medical Center for a presentation and Bonnie mentioned to Ann how we did all this work to set up the spa treatment and dinner and how few nurses took advantage of them. She asked Ann why she thought this was happening. Ann looked at Bonnie.

Bonnie and DAISY as a whole have never forgotten Ann's words: *Don't you get it? It's about the recognition.*

Such a profound lesson in just eight words—simple yet powerful. On a practical level, Ann changed the way we thought and worked. Apparently we hadn't gotten it—not completely—and DAISY wouldn't be anywhere near where we are today if Bonnie hadn't heard Ann—*really listened*—and instead continued to spend half her time trying to set up benefits for nurses that were not really meaningful or relevant to them. We stopped offering the spa treatment and dinner to new hospitals and phased it out at the existing ones. Not one hospital or nurse complained. Mark had been right.

On a more philosophical level, Ann's words affirmed what we did get: the importance of showing appreciation for people so they know the impact they have on us. Not only to nurses but to everyone in our lives. The importance of gratitude—of saying thank you for the little things that others do to make our lives better without any expectation of return. That was what we were honoring in Patrick's memory. That was the DAISY mission.

Fourteen years later, we ran into Ann at a nursing conference. We hadn't seen her in ages. Bonnie told Ann she probably didn't realize what an impact she had on DAISY. That her words supporting our dropping dinners and massages had freed up time for us to reach out to more hospitals, and made a big difference in the expansion of our work. Ann looked at us: "I had no idea I made that kind of difference." It felt to us what it must be like to write a DAISY nomination—a chance to tell someone the impact they had made when they didn't know it. And like a true nurse, she had no idea what a difference she made.

But while Ann may have been right that we didn't get it in one way, we did get it in another—in a way that wasn't even part of the original DAISY idea. Something that, unlike the dinner and spa treatment, nurses have treasured since we introduced it in our second year. Something the American Organization of Nurse Executives found so beautiful and significant that it was the only thing pictured as part of a front-page article on DAISY in its July 2004 newsletter. Something that became symbolic of the relationships nurses have with their patients. Something that delivered a message of recognition in a way no massage or meal ever could. The sculpture that has come to express the very meaning of the DAISY Awards: *The Healer's Touch*.

DAISY HONOREE STORY

Leah R. Bierer, RN
Leah M. Cesaretti, RN
VA Pittsburgh Healthcare System
Pittsburgh, Pennsylvania

At the start of the morning shift, Leah Bierer answered the phone, not knowing she was answering a call from a patient who was expressing suicidal ideation. The patient had the desire and plan to fulfill his thoughts. Leah Bierer was caring, expressing her compassion, and attentively listening to the patient.

While all this was happening, Leah Cesaretti jumped into action by calling the appropriate personnel to do a wellness check on this patient. The patient hung up the phone but Leah B was not giving up on the patient. She called him back and continued to talk to him, assuring him that she cared and was available for the patient. The patient continuously hung up on her, but both Leahs continued to take turns calling the patient, assuring the patient that each one was available and wanted to talk with him.

Leah C took it upon herself to notify his wife, who was unaware that her husband was currently on the phone talking to Leah B about his plan. Leah C was assured by the wife that the patient did not have access to firearms and that they were locked up. After multiple calls and over three hours of phone conversations between both Leahs talking to the patient and expressing their compassion, empathy, caring, and encouraging the patient to seek help from the VA, the patient changed his mind about his plan. He knew he had a rapport with both ladies and could trust them because they cared and listened to his concerns.

I believe if it had not been for these two ladies, things could have ended differently for the patient. Leah B had just completed a 12-hour night shift and stayed a 16-hour shift for this patient. Leah C was coming on, in charge, and demonstrated her leadership skills that can be modeled by all staff at VAPHS. Both of these RNs demonstrated the ICARE principles of VAPHS and deserve to be recognized with the DAISY Award. Thank you for your compassionate service to the Vietnam Vet.

"Having received the DAISY Award reminds me that there are those people out there who understand. It makes the hard days easier. I see The Healer's Touch *on my dresser, and I know the day is going to be okay."*

Michele Robison, RN

The Healer's Touch

The nurse dropped her *Healer's Touch* sculpture. She was so excited she was shaking as we presented it to her along with her DAISY pin and certificate, and it just slipped through her hands. Excitement turned to shock as it cracked into pieces on the floor. She gasped, as did the auditorium applauding her—and if you're among the millions of DAISY Honorees and Nominees, chances are you also gasped. That's how important the *Healer's Touch* has become to the DAISY Awards and the nurses who receive them.

We did not gasp. Before her shock turned to tears, we told the nurse and the audience not to worry; we had another sculpture to replace it. Like each nurse-patient relationship, each *Healer's Touch* is a unique creation. But unlike those relationships, the sculptures are replaceable—a great relief to our honoree and the hundreds of nurses and their family members who have called and emailed over the years, devastated that something happened to their sculpture. Not as many get emotional and call about losing their pins or their certificates. The *Healer's Touch* goes deeper; it has a perpetual essence. We hear countless stories of nurses giving their sculptures places of honor in their homes. As several chief nursing officers told us, the *Healer's Touch* speaks to who they are as human beings—to their compassion and what patients receive from them every day. It's not hyperbole to say it has become a special symbol to nurses. More than 400 hospitals have ordered three-foot-tall versions of the sculptures to grace their healing gardens and lobbies. The *Healer's Touch* also has a spiritual connection to its source: More than 20 gifted artists and their teams in Zimbabwe create them for DAISY all year long to support their entire extended families.

This lasting significance of the *Healer's Touch* sculptures amazes us considering they were not part of the original DAISY idea.

❀ ❀ ❀

In 2002 we knew we wanted to add a permanent gift to the award beyond the pin, certificate, Cinnabons, the dinner and spa treatment—something uniquely DAISY. We didn't know what the gift should be, nor did we plan on it becoming *that* important. We just wanted something memorable to present. What we did know was that we did not want it to be some kind of trophy, no Oscar-like statuette. While some call DAISY the Oscar of nursing, we have never referred to our DAISY Honorees as winners. The DAISY Award is not about winning; it's about gratitude. We wanted a gift of gratitude.

We didn't have to go far to find the right one. Walking through a local gallery, we spotted a sculpture called *Mother and Child*. Carved in

Zimbabwe of serpentine stone, it was a classic design of the country's Shona artists, masters of stone cutting for thousands of years. Both of us remembered it from our travels in southern Africa and felt it perfectly captured and symbolized the nurse-patient relationship: One figure taller than the other but the two inseparable, their arms blending and holding each other up, equal pillars of support. It became even more meaningful when we learned of the profound respect and deep affection the Shona people have for their healers. They are called "treasures" by those they care for, and their well-being and safety is of community-wide importance. This described exactly how everyone

The Healer's Touch made by Shona artists of Zimbabwe

who touches DAISY feels about nurses! We decided to rechristen the mother-child sculptures we would present as *The Healer's Touch* to honor this connection between these worlds. We placed an order with a local gallery and expected to receive them the following year.

Why so long? We needed dozens of them, and the process of carving these stunning sculptures into works of art takes Shona artists almost two weeks to complete. Chisels, mallets, and chasing hammers shape the raw stone into the sculpture's form, proportion, and size. Raspers, water, and waterpapers (a kind of sandpaper) leave it round and smooth for heating and polishing. The entire process takes about two weeks to complete before the artists sign them.

When our first signed *Healer's Touch* sculptures finally arrived in 2003, the gallery packaged them handsomely in black boxes, and we headed to Sonoma Valley Hospital to present one for the first time. The response was like nothing we had seen at a presentation before but would repeat for years to come. We knew we had something special—a piece of art nurses and DAISY could call their own that they also saw as a symbol of the care they provide. As we prepared to ship sculptures to all the hospitals with their awards, we figured we had all systems in place for the foreseeable future. The massage and meal were being phased out. The *Healer's Touch* would become the only gift to go with the pin, certificate, and, of course, the Cinnabons. We had a process in place to get as many as we needed. Like so many times in our journey, we were wrong. After a few years, the production of the *Healer's Touches* created as much anxiety in us as it did joy in the nurses. As DAISY grew, supply was inconsistent, often late, and the production lacked standardization: Every sculpture was a different size and shape. We needed more than we could get, and we needed a better price. We were not sure what to do.

The solution came when we weren't even looking for one and in a place we never expected: the Santa Rosa Plaza Mall.

❈ ❈ ❈

In December 2008, we headed up to Santa Rosa Memorial Hospital to join the nurses for their DAISY presentation. To this day we try to visit as many hospitals as we can, and since this was back when we still provided Cinnabons for the DAISY ceremonies, we headed to the store in Santa Rosa Plaza, around the corner from the hospital, to pick them up. The mall was decked out in full Christmas, but as we headed to the food court our eyes were drawn from the familiar decorations and displays to a kiosk selling, of all things, Shona sculpture. We had never seen a kiosk like it anywhere, and we easily spotted the *Mother and Child* for sale.

We panicked. "Mark!" Bonnie exclaimed. "We'd better buy them all. We don't want the nurses to walk in and think they can just buy them at any kiosk in any mall."

Our surprise continued when we reached the kiosk. The retail price for a single sculpture was less than what we were paying in bulk from the gallery. Granted, the gallery's pieces were from established artists whose work sells in galleries, which also slowed production, but we liked these mall versions even more. They felt substantial—two to three times heavier than the gallery's versions. They seemed to be of equal or better quality too, similar in shape, and all were the eight-inch height we wanted but couldn't consistently get.

As we gathered every *Mother and Child* off the shelves, we started chatting with the woman running the kiosk. She told us a guy named John was the kiosk owner. Bonnie gave her our card and asked if she could have John call us. "Why don't you just talk to him now?" she said as she pulled out her phone and dialed. "John, a couple is buying all your mother and children pieces. You want to talk to them?"

And that's how we met John Reynolds.

John had grown up in South Africa during the apartheid era. A white man, he witnessed the incredible disparity between his family's life and the lives of his black countrymen. This deeply troubled him, as he saw the lives of many black Africans up close while doing volunteer work with his church. He decided to leave South Africa. He found a job in California and made a life for himself, but after several years, he felt unfulfilled. He wasn't giving back, and wanted to do something for the Africans he left behind. So he did something about it. He put some money together, flew back to Zimbabwe, bought a bunch of miscellaneous art and trinkets from the artisans who desperately needed the money, and brought it back to sell in the United States. If it worked, he believed he would help himself and the people he bought it from. The art wasn't an instant hit, but in 1996 John's business found its groove and he opened up a 144-square-foot kiosk in the Santa Rosa Plaza. The same one we came upon on our way to pick up Cinnabons.

Bonnie took the phone and told John about DAISY and what we were looking for. He offered to meet us the next day at his storage unit. "I related to their cause," John recalls. "I'm drawn to people that have a higher purpose than just making money. Their story struck a chord in me. That they lost their Patrick was a strong connection. I lost my father when he was just 56."

John didn't have tables in his storage unit so he had laid all the *Mother and Child* sculptures on the floor before we arrived. They looked like a miniature army of mothers and children. Each one was of the same quality we had cleaned out at the mall. We were impressed and ordered 500 pieces. We could have ordered more, but we wanted to

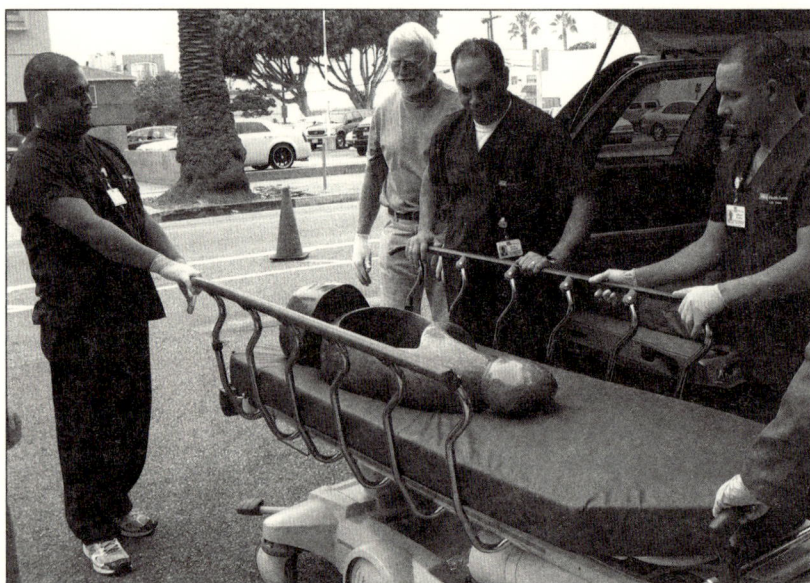

Delivering a large *Healer's Touch* to UCLA Medical Center, Santa Monica, 2010. The three-foot-tall sculptures are bought by organizations for display in their lobbies and healing gardens.

be sure John could deliver. He delivered—every sculpture exactly as promised and on time, the same meticulous consistency and quality as those we saw at his kiosk, and hand-signed by an artist. John also explained to us how unbelievably important that first sale had been to the artists in Zimbabwe.

The year 2008 had been a brutal one in Zimbabwe. The country had been the "bread basket" of Africa, but the government's policies changed all that. In 2008, hyperinflation wasn't simply out of control, it was preposterous. When we met John for the first time that December, Zimbabwe had stopped officially measuring the inflation rate, but estimates had it at 79.6 *billion* percent. Tourism had all but disappeared. The artists John knew were suffering more than his kiosk business could ever help. "DAISY was a lifeline," John says. "It was heartbreaking, but also gratifying. Those first orders saved lives. Today, DAISY is an umbrella of sustenance over the artists—and me."

※ ※ ※

Over the next year or so, Mark was getting tired of being our shipping department on top of running the financial affairs of the Foundation. He spent his days in his office, packing boxes of pins, certificate portfolios, and our beautiful *Healer's Touch* sculptures. We still tried to go to at least the first presentation at every hospital, so we were traveling like crazy. In 2009, we decided to ask John to work for us 10 hours a week doing shipping. Ten hours soon became 15, and then, as John says, "DAISY was on the runway, took off, and started flying." His team in Zimbabwe grew from six to many, many people working together to deliver the thousands of *Healer's Touches* we would come to need. John loves telling stories of the incredible journey these sculptures make to get into our hands so we can get them into the hands of the nurses, and the power he feels when they finally arrive: "The scene is mesmerizing. It's a vast beautiful ocean of *Healer's Touches* lined up and ready to be packaged with care for DAISY Honorees."

That's the operative word: care. Every person involved in the *Healer's Touch* process cares about and for each other. When Judea, one of the supervising artists John had known for 25 years, died from a heart attack in 2018, we were all devastated. But John told us that an uncle who worked with Judea had taken over and would take care of his wife and family. Because that's the culture of the Shona: If something bad happens to any part of their family, others step in to care for them. That's the culture of the nursing profession as well. It's what DAISY has been built on: caring about others and building relationships. After all, we would never be telling this long *Healer's Touch* story if nurses did not care about us enough to tell others—and then tell us what we meant to them when we needed it most in the years following our aggressive discussion in the summer of 2004.

DAISY HONOREE STORY

Oncology Team Snow Day
UCLA Medical Center Santa Monica
Santa Monica, California

A dying 33-year-old father had a final wish, to take his six-year-old daughter to the snow. That is not an easy request in Southern California. Remarkably, in three short days Snow Day happened and was perfect.

The father had endured two years of treatment including a tandem stem cell transplant and moving his family to L.A. His significant other and daughter were always at his side caring, supporting, and loving him. A cure was not to be and he relapsed less than a month after his stem cell transplant. Heartbroken but determined to live for his daughter, he endured several more months of chemotherapy with little response.

One week before Christmas, this father was admitted to the oncology unit, where everyone loved him and his family. This admission, it was clear that time was short. His daughter was a bright star for her father and all those around her. He held the hand of one of his dedicated nurse healers and said, "I want to take my daughter to the snow." As word spread about this dying wish, the compassion and need to go above and beyond took on a life of its own. Oncology staff started calling, emailing, and texting, and Snow Day was born.

Money for the fifteen tons of snow was found from hospital administration. Money was Venmo-ed for tickets to Disney On Ice for the daughter and her aunt. Snow gloves were purchased, Queen Elsa was found (friend of a nurse's daughter) and many nurses and care partners were off buying "snow" stuff. Oncology staff all around were asking, "What can I do?," "Do you need more money?," and "Can we all come?" Staff put their own holiday plans on hold to make this event possible. This day was about more than snow—it was about dreams, compassion, and our love of our oncology patients. No one at UCLA Santa Monica said "no," but instead said, "What can we do to help?"

Night nurses and care partners set their alarms and dragged themselves out of bed after a few hours of sleep to witness this remarkable day. The day shift was staffed up to allow nurses to rotate down to the party. Staff came with their children and dogs, and many from the hospital came to witness this remarkable event: snow in Southern California. One nurse, too busy to come to the party, took her break later in the day and she and the daughter enjoyed an hour playing in the snow. She could not get enough time in the snow. The attending physician paused rounds and the entire team came to the party.

Respiratory therapy was necessary as the patient was on high-flow oxygen. The therapists planned and practiced how to get him outside for several hours, everyone going above and beyond their workday. Queen Elsa arrived at the patient's room and the daughter was speechless—this was her dream come true. Family members changed the father into his Santa suit, placed him in the wheelchair and two respiratory therapists followed him with carts of oxygen tanks.

The Snow Day reinforced for all the oncology staff that our work is messy, difficult, and the most remarkable nursing that one can do. Our hearts were joyful watching them playing in the snow. None of us will ever forget the day that the oncology staff once again made an amazing difference.

The father died on Christmas morning, his significant other at his side and his daughter with family, waiting for Santa.

"I am a patient advocate first and foremost. It was humbling and special to be honored by my patients. It is very rewarding to be able to be a positive influence in someone's life."

Debbie Zahren Edwards, BSN, RN, CRNI, RN-BC

A Broken Promise

B onnie's mom was Bea Wain, a big-name big band and radio singer in the 1930s and '40s. (Fun fact: She was the first artist to record "Over the Rainbow," but MGM refused to release it until *The Wizard of Oz* opened and then only released the Judy Garland version.) Mom, or Beazer as Mark called her, passed away in 2017 at the age of 100. Before she died, we went down regularly to see her in Beverly Hills. We would take her out for a steak dinner at the Porterhouse Grill, because that's pretty much all she ate—nothing but meat. No vegetables. No soup. Maybe eggs.

Late one afternoon in 2004, we were out for one of our steak dinners together when a good-looking young waiter introduced himself. With the restaurant mostly empty, Bonnie started making small talk. His name was Damian and like so many Los Angeles waiters, he was trying to make a go of it as an actor in Hollywood. The rest of his story was not so typical. Two years earlier, Damian had left his pregnant wife, Christa, behind in Denver to come to L.A. to study acting and start auditioning. For their anniversary, Christa came to visit, and at just 23 weeks pregnant went into labor and gave birth to their baby boy, Cole. He was whisked to Children's Hospital of Los Angeles. Cole lived all of his first months in the NICU and endured 12 surgeries over most of his first two years. But today Cole was doing great—a happy and energetic kid.

We were in tears as Damian finished his story. Then Bonnie said, "Tell me about the nurses." Damian's face lit up. He said he didn't know what he would have done without their nurses. They basically were Christa's and his family in L.A., given none of their actual family lived in California. "They have been everything to us."

Bonnie smiled. "Would you like to say thank you?"

We explained DAISY to Damian, and he could not have been more excited about the idea of honoring Cole's nurse, Lisa. The next day, Bonnie called the chief nursing officer at Children's Hospital Los Angeles. She got voice mail. "This is Mary Dee Hacker . . ." Bonnie left a message relating the family's desire to say thank you to the nurses who cared for their son and to honor those nurses and many more by bringing DAISY into the hospital. She hung up the phone and wondered how long it would take to hear back—or even if she would. *These calls take time and follow-up,* she thought to herself, remembering what she learned from Bonnie Lasky.

Five minutes later, our phone rang. "Hi Bonnie, this is Mary Dee Hacker. I know exactly who you are. We would love to have the DAISY Award at Children's Hospital Los Angeles." Weeks later, Children's

Hospital Los Angeles became our 27th DAISY hospital. Just over a year after making it, Bonnie had broken her promise to Mark to stop at 50 hospitals—a promise neither of us wanted to keep anymore. Not that we could, even if we did want to keep it. Slowly but surely, DAISY was taking on a life of its own.

* * *

"I don't think it was within five minutes, but let's stick with that," says Mary Dee, who retired from Children's Hospital Los Angeles in 2017. She had known about DAISY because it launched in California, and just before Bonnie called, Mary Dee had dinner with Ann Dechairo-Marino, the chief nursing officer at Northridge Medical Center. Ann was the one the year before who asked if we got it, reminded us that it's about the recognition, and compelled us to ditch the dinner and spa treatment gifts. Ann had told Mary Dee all about DAISY.

"The world of CNOs is pretty tight," Mary Dee says. "Back in those days in particular, we all really counted on each other to be our sources of wisdom and clarification and information. To hear about an opportunity to say thank you to the nurses at Children's Hospital, whose hearts are as big as their intelligence—and to have that thank-you coming from outside of us, was something that I considered to be of paramount importance. And the idea of tying it back to the families and children we serve was a dimension that we didn't have in our toolbox at Children's Hospital Los Angeles. We can create all kinds of things within our organization, and we do. But the most meaningful things have always come from people on the outside who say, 'I want to help honor that.' They see what I can't. I'm not watching nurses at three o'clock in the morning. I can't be in every room. So the decision to bring in DAISY wasn't complicated. It was: 'Yes, please, help me thank and appreciate these people who come to their jobs each day with a commitment to help from both a clinical standpoint, as well as from a human connection standpoint.'" You can never thank people enough in life, but this is especially true for nurses who every day come to work in emotionally challenging environments. No matter where they are, how big the organization, and who they serve, nurses are, as Mary Dee says, "forever present. They are with patients and families during the most challenging times of their lives, and they are there with clinical knowledge and a caring heart."

There was another reason that made Mary Dee believe that DAISY would be a perfect fit for the culture of Children's Hospital Los Angeles: Its devotion to the concept of family- or patient-centered care, that is, listening to, involving, and informing patients when it comes to their care and clinical decisions. Mary Dee first read about this concept when she was an undergraduate student in Minnesota in the late 1960s. The work came out of Children's Hospital Los Angeles but was dismissed as West Coast "crazy" by many of her nursing teachers and colleagues. "Back in those days, it was very much believed that nursing was more of a technical expertise rather than a caring art. But Children's Hospital Los Angeles has clearly understood and embraced a sense of humanity in providing care. DAISY not only fit our culture really well but enhanced it."

That Mary Dee believed this and got the power of recognition and gratitude—and got that DAISY got it, too—energized all of us. We sprang into action. We arranged for the first DAISY Award at Children's Hospital Los Angeles to be given in October 2004 to Cole's nurse, Lisa Coffman. Simultaneously, Mary Dee looked for someone to run DAISY who had the time and would embrace its value, even if that value was just beginning to be understood by nurses and hospitals. As it so happened that the day Mary Dee announced to her team she was bringing DAISY in, she was having a retirement party for Marion Antoku. A nurse at Children's for 40-plus years, Marion had also been Mary Dee's manager when she was starting out. Mary Dee knew Marion would do a fabulous job running DAISY, connect to it, and have time to do it right.

It was Marion who greeted us in the lobby when we arrived at the hospital with Damian, Christa, and Cole for the first award. She handed us our security badges and walked with us toward the room where the presentation would take place. We thought Cole would be screaming, crying, and a nervous wreck, not wanting to be at the place he had been in and out of constantly for two years. Wrong. Cole was just as Damian described him: happy and energetic. Being at Children's was like he was at the playground. He kept moving and smiling, pointing out things on the wall and showing us rooms and, of course, the toy bins.

And then we got to the room for the presentation and Cole saw Lisa. He ran across the floor to her and gave her the biggest hug. The rest of the event was a beautiful and joyful celebration. All the powers that be at Children's Hospital Los Angeles were there. We left knowing DAISY was in the best hands. But what lingers in our memory today was that hug from little Cole to his nurse, Lisa.

As we always say, nurses give the best hugs but when those hugs meet the hug of a grateful and loving child, words fail to capture the feeling.

Lisa Coffman's name was the first added to a DAISY Award plaque that would be permanently mounted in a public hallway at Children's Hospital Los Angeles with room to add many more names. To find those names for the next awards, Mary Dee and Marion established a committee and put out a call for nominations. Moving forward, they decided that as at many hospitals, the awards would be given as surprises to the nurses. But Children's extended that surprise to everyone in the units where the nurses worked. Mary Dee and Marion also decided to invite the honoree's family members to make the surprise even more powerful—a complicated process but so worth it for the DAISY Honorees in their opinion. What neither Mary Dee nor Marion counted on was that the hospital would get so many nominations that the selection committee of nurses was overwhelmed by its success.

"I think that DAISY grew organically in hospitals in its first years, so it took a while for the communication and the value of it to be shared," recalls Mary Dee, who years later joined our board. "CNOs are busy, but my lens was that anything I can do to raise nurses up and say thank you, I want to be doing." Turns out, others had started to see through that same lens and understand the importance of building a culture of recognition in the organization. This came into sharper focus for us that same fall when DAISY received its first cold call.

❄ ❄ ❄

"This is Ann Evans," the voice on the other end of the phone said as soon as Bonnie picked up the phone. "Are you for real?" Anyone who knows Ann knows this is exactly what she said. Ann was then vice president and chief of patient care services at Tallahassee Memorial Hospital and cold-called us after reading about DAISY in the July 2004 American Organization of Nurse Executives (AONE) newsletter. Ann had been president of the American Association of Critical-Care Nurses (AACN). She was well aware of the landmark work AACN was undertaking on the essentials of a healthy work environment, one of which was meaningful recognition of nurses. But even before AACN published their research in 2005, Ann saw something meaningful in the recognition DAISY offered. After assuring her we indeed were for real and having a delightful conversation, we booked a flight to Florida to get DAISY going. And very soon, it was going.

Despite the Mary Dee and Ann Evans experiences, in early 2005 it didn't look like Bonnie was going to break her promise to Mark. We added fewer hospitals in 2004 (10) than in 2003 (11) and finished the year with a total of 28. But what started with Mary Dee and Ann Evans really started to roll in the next few years. Sure, Bonnie was still cold calling, but more and more people answered those calls to action, including donors. Shortly after meeting Damian, Bonnie ran into her former assistant from her advertising days, Jonathan Weedman, who had become the head of the Wells Fargo Foundation in Los Angeles. She explained DAISY and asked if he wanted to sponsor the awards at Children's Hospital for a $1,000 donation to cover the costs. He gave us $2,000 and told us to always ask for double what something costs when dealing with a corporate sponsor—that way even if you can't use it to spread more good in the world, you can still cover what you need if you get less!

The chance encounter with Jonathan underscored for us once again the power of lasting relationships—not just for DAISY but for life in general. That was certainly true for the health of DAISY. Our relationships with nurses and their relationships with each other were fundamental to DAISY's growth.

Ann Evans eventually brought dozens of hospitals and a few industry partners to DAISY, and she joined our board. Mary Dee Hacker also joined our board and didn't just build the future for

DAISY at Children's. She made it her mission to get other children's hospitals to adopt DAISY. "CNOs of the children's hospitals in the country meet twice a year together, and it's a really tight community," Mary Dee says. "We share practice. We strive hard to reduce harm and injury and improve care. So we're collaborative, not competitive, and at those meetings, I talked about the DAISY Award and recognition, and I invited those CNOs to become part of it and that was effective. It was that simple."

In May 2005, Beth Heyman, who ran DAISY at Health Alliance of Greater Cincinnati, wrote to us after our visit to talk about and present the DAISY Award at one of her hospitals: "I am still caught up in the emotional (both personal and professional) high you brought to Cincinnati. I thank you for your time and commitment to something you obviously believe in with your hearts. YOU made ME proud to be a nurse! If I lived closer to you I would give you all my time for your cause to use in any way you needed." She committed to getting us 10 more hospital contacts in Ohio and beyond. She said she, her family, and her nursing network had already pitched DAISY to several hospitals in Chicago. She was ready to "nudge," she said. "I am taking up the cause." (Beth later became dean of the Galen College of Nursing in Cincinnati and joined our board. In 2007, she launched the discussion that later led to DAISY adding nursing faculty to our awards: "Someone had to teach those nurses who took such great care of your son Patrick.")

In 2006, Susan Grant, who had been the chief nursing officer at the University of Washington Medical Center when we presented our first DAISY Award, became the system chief nurse executive at Emory Health in Atlanta and quickly brought DAISY to all three hospitals in the system at the time. "In healthcare, we know very well as nurses, as physicians, as administrators, we do not build the patient and family voice into everything we do," Susan says. "We look through the lens of an administrator or a healthcare professional and that's not always a lens that considers what patients and families think. The whole goal for my being brought into Emory was advancing patient- and family-centered care and elevating nursing to achieve Magnet designation in our different hospitals. But there wasn't really a framework for professional practice that was consistently applied across the hospitals. So I used DAISY as a tool for people to start to paint the canvas of what professional practice looks like."

To achieve this, Susan opened up DAISY nominations from not only patients and families, but also staff and other professionals. She and other administrators would read those nominations out loud to nursing staff across the hospitals so they could hear what professional practice looks like. She made meaningful recognition part of Emory's transformation model. Like we have heard from so many chief nursing officers, DAISY gave Susan a genuine story rather than just numbers from satisfaction surveys that don't tell you anything about what those numbers mean. Susan wasn't looking for data or compliance numbers. She was looking for something that nurses could build on and grow and learn from.

"I could talk about holding ourselves to high standards of care, using the Magnet framework," Susan says. "But those are just words from a nurse administrator. The nurses probably are thinking, 'I know she believes in what she's talking about and it sounds really good, but I have no idea what that actually means or looks like in practice.' Using the DAISY nominations and reading them as exemplars of outstanding nursing practice that were in the words of patients and of families—in the words of their colleagues—that showed what outstanding practice actually looks like. . . . Everybody got it and could relate to it. And before you knew it there were nursing practice councils on units that were holding themselves to that vision. DAISY empowers nurses to kind of carry that vision and continue to evolve it instead of it being this top-down nurse administrator saying, 'Here, I'm going to tell you how to do this and what it's going to look like.' Nurses create it."

Stories like Susan's, Mary Dee's, Beth's, and Ann Evans's are the main reason that after adding only 49 hospitals in its first five years, DAISY added 133 in its next two. Every hospital we added brought another one, two, five—not just from its own system but thanks to the relationships between nurses. Nurses were also moving from hospital to hospital and bringing DAISY with them. As Susan said, DAISY was being *owned* by the nurses, and that could not have delighted us more.

It was why when we added our 50th hospital in January 2006, we knew we couldn't stop, Bonnie's promise to Mark notwithstanding. We sailed past 50 hospitals to more than 100 by mid-2007.

Problem was, we had no infrastructure, no database, to support all this growth. Suddenly we felt like we were drowning. It was 2007. DAISY was approaching 200 hospitals. Mark was doing all our shipping from a guest room in our house. Bonnie was doing the paperwork by hand from another room we converted to an office. All day long she heard his tape gun going, packing pins, certificate portfolios, and *Healer's Touch* sculptures. It was a happy sound . . . and completely overwhelming. Something had to give or we never would have made it to 2008 and met John Reynolds in that mall. DAISY was getting expensive—more expensive than we could possibly sustain even with the generosity of our donors. We were just full-time volunteers, paying for our own travel and most DAISY expenses. If we didn't do something, DAISY would soon be a victim of its own success.

While we built our board and figured out what to do, the nurses not only drove DAISY forward, they lifted us up with their words and their stories of compassionate care.

DAISY HONOREE STORY

Emily J. Cooper, RN
VA Lexington Health Care System
Lexington, Kentucky

Emily Cooper has been an asset to this hospital for several years. Starting out as a student nurse tech many years ago, working part-time as a bedside ICU RN, and even working in the ER, she has grown into an inspirational RN for all of us to aspire to be like. She is a leader whom I can trust professionally because of her critical thinking skills as well as her love and compassion for our veterans and staff.

Emily has had to hire several nurses to fill the holes within our staffing. Recently, to overcome the issues of the lack of education in our critical care units, she develop[ed] new and fun ways to keep our bedside nurses engaged in the care of the Veterans. For example, she created a tool that allowed us to follow the hypoglycemic protocol closer, document, and ensure that the protocol was followed correctly. Without this, glycemic events would remain in the forefront of our struggle with Veterans. She has tirelessly fought to maintain the reputation and high integrity of critical care.

With only new staff members scheduled, Emily has volunteered to stay over her shift a few hours so that the ICU was covered with a strong critical care nurse. She has worked the floor numerous times to be that resource and helping hand. It is always for the safety of the Veterans, making sure that they are given proper care and attention. Only extraordinary nurses do the things she has done for her Veterans, such as supplying items for our bereavement cart for families of our hospice or comfort patients.

Education has been Emily's passion since stepping into the position of nurse manager. She has developed a plan for our night shift nurses to get their critical skills classes/refreshers regularly so they may remain confident in their skills at the bedside. She wants to make sure the nurses know *how* to critically think on their own for the future. Not only is she someone we can all turn to for advice or "an extra set of eyes"; she is someone that has the foresight in the care of her Veterans due to her extensive experience.

Just recently, Emily was in the middle of a meeting with a coworker and heard the CODE BLUE announcement overhead. She stopped what she was doing, jumped up, and ran onto the unit to assist. Emily saw that there were plenty of hands in the room, and she stepped back. Emily assisted by being a runner and priming the LEVEL 1 rapid transfuser to be ready for blood. She delegated tasks and even made sure that the rest of the unit was running smoothly during the chaos of the CODE BLUE. When all resuscitation efforts were exhausted, they called the time of death. After a quick debrief, Emily went back into the patient's room and started to clean him up. She could have easily watched her staff remove all of his lines and bathe him, but she jumped right in and assisted. Emily focuses on Veteran-centered care every minute of each shift. It says something when your nurse manager will do anything to assist her staff when they are busy or in a bind.

For the past six months, Emily Cooper has been the driving force behind the changes on and surrounding our Critical Care. Emily's leadership is behind our complete departmental turnaround. She brought the staff together by communicating her vision for Critical Care's future and the role we would play in it.

Emily has taught us, fought for us, stood side by side with us, and cried with us. She is constantly looking at ways to improve not only our unit but us as nurses and as people, helping us have a healthy work-life balance. Emily has also worked very hard to improve the work satisfaction of her staff members. Many of our nurses have been able to receive their Nurse III because of her drive to assist them in that cause.

There aren't many leaders in this world like Emily. She would give you the shirt off her back. Emily is more than our boss. She is our confidant, our voice, our leader, and most importantly, our friend. We are all so thankful for having Emily over our Critical Care units. She is willing to do anything for anyone. Her selflessness and compassion have made her the most deserving nurse for the DAISY Award. There is no one in this world like her. Critical Care is fortunate to have an organically made nurse manager as our leader.

"Though I honestly don't feel like what I did was extraordinary, receiving the award was probably the most touching acknowledgment I will ever receive as a nurse."

Rebecca Johnson, RN

The Power of Stories and Gratitude

I grew up on a dairy farm with seven siblings. My parents said if we wanted to go on to college we would have to pay our own way. Wanting to be a nurse from childhood, I worked as a nurse aide for several years and saved my money to go to nursing school. When I went to pay my admissions fee, I found they had raised tuition significantly, and I didn't have enough money to enter the program. My dad said he would somehow work something out to get the money. A few *weeks later, he took me back to the school and put down the remaining money needed. It was only when we got home that I realized he and Mother had sold our prize milk cow to get the money. The cow's name was Daisy. When I heard Bonnie and Mark's story, I loved the idea of yet another way to recognize my nursing staff. But the name Daisy held a special place in my heart.*

We have loved that story since the day we heard Jane Swaim, then the chief nursing officer at St. Elizabeth's Healthcare, tell it to us in 2007. Truth is, we had to reach out to her to get the story again when we were writing this book. We were bad at recording any stories back then. We didn't start featuring DAISY Honorees and their nominations on our website until that same year. Our early nomination forms and many of those from our partner hospitals didn't have much room for those stories, either. Some of them were just a small sheet of paper you tore from a pad. To help sustain our program, we asked our participating hospitals to create their own criteria that fit their culture under the banner of compassionate care, which is what DAISY was established to recognize. So many of the hospitals' criteria were things like positive attitude, meeting patient and family needs, collaborating with the healthcare team, and interpersonal skills. But then the form had just a line or three for an explanation. They read, well, clinically. Some didn't even use the word compassion, despite our mission. As a result, a lot of the early nominations went something like, "Mary was a wonderful nurse. She went above and beyond to take care of us during this time."

We didn't get the rich details we have today until we evolved the forms, and then pushed every hospital to make stories the priority. Honestly, we weren't very good at pushing for nominations, let alone stories, in our first years. In fact, the nurses were the ones who pointed the way for much of what we include when organizations sign up for DAISY. First came the idea for a banner, from Providence St. Vincent's Hospital in Portland, Oregon. After Bonnie stopped crying the first time she saw it, we started working on giving one to all our hospitals. Then a hospital in Michigan started giving a pin, which they designed, to every nurse who got a nomination. Being trained in advertising and marketing, we also shared that idea. (Bonnie prefers that Mark use the

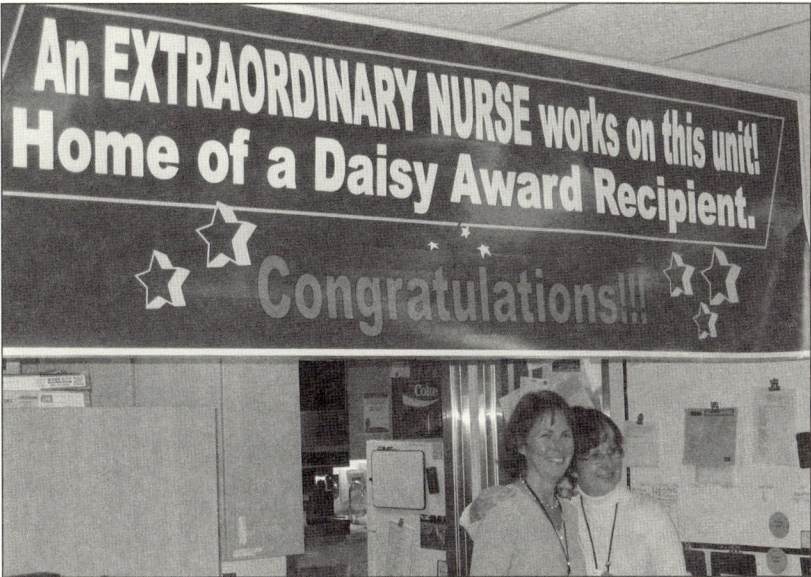

Providence St. Vincent's Hospital in Portland, OR created the first DAISY banner in 2004. They may have spelled DAISY lowercase, but Bonnie still cried tears of joy when she saw it.

"Stolen" Idea: Our first version of the now-coveted DAISY banner displayed at a DAISY Award presentation at Cincinnati Children's Hospital, 2006

term "share" rather than "stole" but the result was the same. Later, we share-stole that same hospital's design for a pin for nurses who had been nominated several times.)

A real turning point for us was when we visited OSF Saint Francis Medical Center in Peoria, Illinois, which was getting thousands of nominations a year. (We knew because they kept ordering nominee pins.) We asked how they were doing it. The nurses walked us into a patient room and there was a sign with daisies and a big bold headline: THANK YOUR NURSE. Below that the words continued: FOR OUTSTANDING CARE. It then asked people to complete a DAISY Award nomination form and where to find it. Bonnie's a born and bred New Yorker, and even she thought this was pushy. But then we realized maybe we were being too reserved. Even if a sign like that didn't lead to a nomination, it could at least lead to a thank-you, which we much later realized *our own materials did not say*. Yes, it was a real head-slapping moment in DAISY's existence to recognize our first signs did not say THANK YOUR NURSE—in spite of the fact that we were so grateful, and countless nurses told us DAISY was creating a culture of gratitude as well as recognition. It even built bridges between mortal enemies: One nurse told us that despite being a proud Michigan State Spartan, the DAISY Award from her colleagues at the University of Michigan hospital made "a place in [her] heart for those of you who are Wolverines."

Today we can't say thank you enough to nurses for being nurses, even if those nurses think that they are "not doing anything special." So we thank them for "just doing your job." For making the world a better place by staying true to the importance of caring in healing—a principle to which nurses commit when they join this noble profession. But in 2007, we were just waking up to the larger importance of saying thank you along with the power of the nomination stories.

Like we said, however, many nurses and more and more hospitals like OSF Saint Francis already understood this. They were using DAISY to enhance and even build their cultures of recognition and gratitude by honoring more than just clinical excellence or some management-selected employee-of-the-month program. They understood the power of stories describing compassionate care. If we needed more of a reminder of just how powerful those DAISY stories and moments of gratitude had become, around the same time as we heard the Daisy cow story, Susan Grant invited us to Emory for a special event.

❋ ❋ ❋

Susan knew we'd come. We tried to attend every event we were invited to (and many we weren't), and we never missed an opportunity to get to Atlanta, because it meant seeing Tena and Riley, who lived there. But Susan had planned something new that made this visit even more exciting. After a year of presenting DAISY Awards at Emory's three hospitals, she arranged for a breakfast with the honorees, many of whom did not know each other and had never met us. They were, however, used to Susan and other leaders reading DAISY nominations aloud as part of developing Emory's professional best practices.

But if the nurses thought that Susan was going to read their stories at the breakfast, they were wrong. As we gathered around the table, Susan asked the nurses themselves to go around the room and tell everyone what they were nominated for. We weren't surprised what happened next.

One of the biggest changes from DAISY's first years had been the willingness of nurses to nominate each other for the DAISY Awards. We got exactly zero nominations from nurses at our first hospital. That changed as they saw the value in the meaningful recognition DAISY offered. Nurses may not see themselves as unsung heroes, but more and more they saw it in each other, especially in the smallest details. They know that little things can make a big difference in their patients' care and outcomes, because there are no little things to patients when it comes to their care and outcomes.

What had *not* changed—and this remains true to this day—was what we captured in how we say thank you to nurses: They are not only shocked by their nominations but feel they have done nothing special to earn them. Nurses feel they're doing this good work because it's who they are. They may be proud of their DAISY Awards, but pride doesn't make them see what they did as impressive, or great at talking about it. That inability was on full display at Emory that morning. After the first nurse self-consciously told her story of being nominated by her patient, the nurse who followed said, "Wow, that's an incredible story. I didn't do anything like that." When she was done, the third nurse said. "Well of course you both got the DAISY Award. I didn't do anything like them. . . . " And so it went. All the way around the room—every nurse just as self-effacing as the last.

Their stories that morning varied in the size and scope of their compassionate care: some grand gestures, some moments of profound intimacy; some acts that happened over the course of an hour, some that played out over weeks and months. Still not one of those nurses saw themselves as doing anything impressive—anything more than what they do every day. But by the time the last nurse spoke, they had to know the emotion that their stories elicited in the room, and that the admiration for them was profound. Everyone at the table was in tears. Okay, Susan cries when you say hello to her, but this time we and all the nurses were with her. They had to know how much they had made a difference. What they might not have known is how much they—and hundreds before them—had been making a difference to *us*.

The certificate each DAISY Honoree receives reads: "In deep appreciation of all you do, who you are, and the incredibly meaningful difference you make in the lives of so many people." We accept that many of our honorees have no idea how special they were to their patients, how much they have made a difference to patients and to other nurses. We can't try to convince them any more than we already have. But we can tell them what a difference their stories and words made to us.

As we worked to figure out the next chapter in DAISY's story, it was stories like those we heard at Emory and words of thanks from the DAISY Honorees across the country that kept us going—and opened us up to changing our story and the entire way DAISY operated.

※ ※ ※

One nurse gave a shave and a haircut to a homeless man after he passed away so that his parents, who hadn't seen him in several years, would see him for who he was and not what he had become.

Shining the Light on All the Right

One nurse washed the hair of a teenage girl so she could look nice when her friends came to visit her in the hospital.

One helped a suicidal patient see clearly.

One painted a snowy picture of the community church and put up Christmas decorations for the patient who was that church's pastor and was lonely for his congregation during the holiday.

One made sure "Tigger" and "Bun Bun" were in the recovery room when a young patient woke up from surgery.

One pushed a patient to fight through the pain and get out of bed and do his exercises after open heart surgery; came back on her day off and refused to leave until he got out of bed; and was waiting for him with a hug when he reached the end of the hall weeks later.

One helped a seven-year-old through a bone marrow transplant.

One brought in her son to play the violin for a patient who loved music.

One went through the garbage in the basement to find a patient's treasure when environmental services thought it was trash.

One snuck in a terminal patient's golden retriever so he could say goodbye to his best friend and companion of 11 years.

One made sure there was always clothes for patients who lacked them.

One gave a patient the sneakers off his feet.

One gave a man a cross when he most needed it.

One—and this is one of Mark's favorites—checked with the doctor and then went to the store for some gin and vermouth to make the perfect martini so a couple, married for 64 years, could enjoy a drink together while the wife was in the hospital.

One nurse put all these DAISY moments and countless more in perspective for us: "It's the small things that you do every day, the things you take for granted that matter so much. It's taking the time to be with parents when you are way behind on your paperwork. It's being a friend and support system to a very young family, helping a mom understand that it's okay for her baby to leave this world and then have her tell you that you made it bearable for her. It's helping the sibling of a baby understand why their brother or sister is sick. It could be as simple as starting an IV for another nurse. At that moment you become their heroes."

And ours.

Those examples we listed are of course just fragments of stories we've heard about the work of DAISY Honorees, almost all of them from the early years of DAISY that revealed the impact nurses had on their patients. They came to us long before we asked for them for our records and our website. They also held us together the first eight years along with the letters we got from those nurses thanking us for the DAISY Award. We got form letters from the places we donated to that support ITP research and patients, but we received hundreds of handwritten heartfelt thank-you's from nurses. Those and the memory of Patrick drove us forward, each one like a hug in the mail. Every summer when Riley came to visit, she would make scrapbooks of them. Stacks of them filled Mark's office, and do to this day.

We also started getting scrapbooks from hospitals and nurses too, many with daisies and hand-colored decorations on their pages. The first really big scrapbook we got was from Children's Hospital Los Angeles from Mary Dee's staff. Memorial Sloan Kettering Cancer Center in New York City sent us a photo book they made online with pictures from their first award, too, something they later did for every nurse. The chief nursing officer at San Francisco General had the scrapbook her nurses maintained of all their DAISY Award honorees on the table outside her office. It was the only thing the nurses who came in to interview with her could look at.

One from Mercy San Juan Medical Center in Sacramento given to us in 2004 had a picture of Patrick on the cover and these words beneath it: "Patrick's wings have lifted many a weary nurse's spirit."

The power of these words did more than just make us emotional. They did more than help us fight through the years we struggled. They did more than strengthen our resolve. They made us change our focus. Until 2005, DAISY still listed ITP organizations we supported in our newsletters. But as the overwhelming response from the nurses we knew and the thousands we did not filled our home, their words showed us not only what DAISY meant to them but also how DAISY worked for

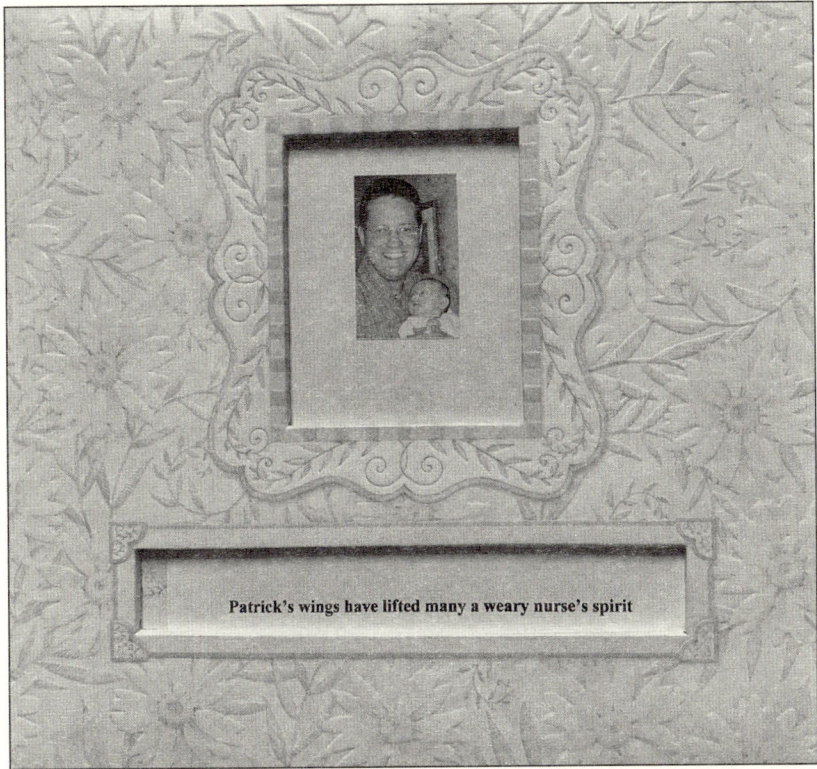

Patrick's wings have lifted many a weary nurse's spirit

"Patrick's wings have lifted many a weary nurse's spirit." The cover of a scrapbook given to us by Mercy San Juan Medical Center, Sacramento, 2004

them, and what was of value to them. The nurses were refining DAISY for us, bringing it front and center. We needed to be all in on the DAISY Awards; we had to focus on the nurses and drop almost everything else. So while we occasionally supported ITP causes personally—not as DAISY—after 2005, DAISY effectively became about the nurses that year.

Not that nurses weren't always our love. (Why else would Bonnie spend so much time cold calling and arranging gifts?) But after a bumpy start, the nurses had gone from *a* focus to *the* focus. Nurses owned DAISY; we were the facilitators. The 2007 DAISY brochure that replaced our homemade newsletter captured this complete swing to nurses:

Since DAISY's inception, we've found ourselves focusing more of our resources, time, and frankly, affection on the DAISY Award than on the other goals. The level of acceptance and appreciation by hospitals has astounded and gratified us. Hospital administrators view the DAISY Award not only as a way to acknowledge outstanding nursing, but also as a strategic tool in managing the nurse shortage that threatens the heart of our healthcare system. Nurses who experienced DAISY presentations are moved and motivated by them. We are very proud of the program's accomplishments for nurses and will work to continue its expansion into more and more hospitals. Patrick would've loved this!

Patrick would also have loved that DAISY was growing more than ever before in 2007, now approaching 200 hospitals and 1,500 DAISY presentations a year. What Patrick would not have loved was the fact that even if we didn't grow any more, we would soon run out of money. We were giving our program as a gift to our hospitals and doing some creative fundraising to add to the significant amount of money we were spending out of our own pocket, like hosting a grape harvest wine weekend at our home for two couples that we sold at an auction every year. But it was hard work. We had tapped our own networks for too long. And we still didn't know that many people in the healthcare industry who would donate. Something had to change.

❁ ❁ ❁

Evidence for our statement about how nurse leaders viewed DAISY was not merely anecdotal. In 2007, we knew dozens of hospitals saw DAISY as beneficial for retention, recruitment, morale, and more. With DAISY growing so rapidly, the year before we had decided to do a detailed survey of our hospital partners to better understand them and how and why they were using the program. We sent a DAISY Award questionnaire to all our hospitals. The eight-page survey asked questions like how frequently they gave out the DAISY Award, how many they had given in the past year, what criteria the hospital used, who could nominate the nurses, whether the hospital had Magnet designation, whether it used the banner we were then providing to them, how DAISY supported the hospital's values, and if we were beneficial for retention. We also asked to see their nomination forms. We received more than 100 responses.

As we combed through them all, we were gratified that so many engaged with DAISY on a deeper level, while the responses from the few that struggled to sustain DAISY confirmed what we suspected: They didn't have the awards embedded in their culture, something we had stressed almost since the beginning. Overall, few of the answers surprised us, except the answers on page six, which focused on our future. Actually, we thought the questions would surprise the hospitals first. Not the one at the top of the page that asked if they planned to continue the DAISY Award in 2007. Even hospitals struggling to embed the award were still committed to DAISY, which has been the case throughout our existence. Only one hospital had dropped the program by 2006, and we have maintained a high retention rate in our first 20 years: excluding hospitals that have closed or merged with others, 96 percent of the more than 4,000 organizations that started presenting the DAISY Award still do.

No, the most surprising question was actually preceded by a one-paragraph explanation under the bold, underlined header "Finally . . . ":

A number of our hospitals have asked us how we fund The DAISY Award and how they might be supportive. We are quite creative with our fundraising. Today, we have been able to support the program financially with the help of Family and Corporate Sponsors so we can provide the program to you at no charge. However, now that we are expanding so rapidly and have a long-term plan for The DAISY Award's growth, we may at some time in the future ask you to help us by contributing to the cost of The DAISY Award at your hospital or directing us to a Sponsor who can underwrite the cost for you. So we would appreciate your insight by answering just a few more questions.

The first question asked how much money chief nursing officers felt would be a reasonable contribution to help us keep the award going at their hospitals. The second asked how long it would take to get that contribution approved in their budgets. We stressed that we were not asking for commitment, simply trying to gauge the hospitals' interest and ability to support the program in the future. We gave them choices of $1,000, $2,000, and $5,000 or more a year as well as the ability to say they couldn't contribute.

Bonnie thought few would say they would pay for something they had been getting for free since the beginning. She was concerned that asking organizations to pay was a violation of our mission and the trust nurse leaders had put in us. She had said as much to her friend Lynne Doll, who had sponsored our third hospital, Cedars-Sinai in Los Angeles. Lynne had introduced UnitedHealthcare as a corporate sponsor for select hospitals they wanted to support. But the company wanted the hospitals to pay for DAISY after one year of corporate sponsorship. That had launched the conversation of the hospitals paying, but Bonnie told the board she didn't like asking, nor did she believe anyone would pay. But she also knew we had no choice unless she wanted to go into full-blown fundraiser mode (which she surely did not). DAISY was growing unsustainably in the hands of the nurses, but we couldn't support them much longer with us paying—a big reason she thought so many of them were signing up. "I didn't want to start charging them because I had worked so hard to get them," Bonnie recalls. "I made all those cold calls. I had been up against people saying, 'Are you for real? Nurses don't need it.' We had gotten all these hospitals to take the program, and I was afraid it would look like a bait and switch."

We got that it was about the recognition, but did nurses and hospitals value that recognition enough to completely reverse how it was funded? Mark had already reversed his opinion. At the time of our aggressive discussion three years earlier, he had wanted to control growth. "And thankfully we did a pretty crappy job of it," he admits, because DAISY was poised to keep growing and growing and growing. Now Mark said if we wanted to grow, we should *grow*—more than just the organic word-of-mouth growth we were experiencing. We knew there was an opportunity to make DAISY bigger than we ever imagined, but we needed to be more strategic. We needed help and support to seize that opportunity. The worst thing that could happen would be having to start turning nurses away and not be able to provide. Bonnie had stopped doing cold calls, but we were getting more calls than we could possibly handle or afford. Mark the entrepreneur had built an organization and said it clearly to Bonnie: "We need to run DAISY like a business." A growing one, not the struggling one from a few years ago. We had zero customer acquisition costs, but we needed help with customer service and fulfillment. We needed a database and a CFO. And we needed money. Would the hospitals be willing to pay?

When the answers to the question about shifting the financial responsibility to the hospitals came in, none—not even the struggling hospitals—checked the box beside "Sorry, we cannot contribute anything." Most of them said they would contribute $2,000—more than we would need to provide them with a monthly award. Some said they would pay more. They saw our value. But Bonnie still took some convincing to shift her mindset—these answers on our questionnaire weren't commitments to pay, just promises. Who finally convinced Bonnie to do so, told us what we needed to do, and then helped us change our story for good? A nurse, of course—the head of one of America's most prestigious nursing organizations. The first organization to help us completely understand the value in our concept and how far we had come from just wanting to say thank you to nurses for the extraordinary care we experienced during Our Patrick's hospitalization in 1999.

DAISY HONOREE STORY

Nicolette Muro, BSN, RN

NYU Langone Hospital – Brooklyn
Brooklyn, New York

Nicolette is very special. She is a huge power force of encouragement, bravery, and love. During my stay at the hospital, she made sure the patient and her rights came first—even when the patient was stubborn, she still helped and was always supporting them. As her patient, she tended to me both physically and mentally. Not many have the time to actually console people mentally due to the workload and stress in her line of work. But she did for me, deeply. She heard my every struggle and the constant blame I put on myself for my condition, and assured me every time things would get better and to not rush them—to especially not blame myself or put myself down because this was out of my control.

What I will take away mostly from my stay was her standing up for me. After so long of many struggles in life, Nicolette made me feel like my voice was heard finally. She made sure I felt comfortable as a patient and never made me feel like I was anything less, because of her charisma. Even when I cried and was giving up, she got me back up. She gave me a sense of life again when I felt so lost, and [made me feel] like I finally mattered. She made my stay in a hospital for the first time in my whole life enjoyable. I have always been to hospitals but being in her unit and care just made me give life a second chance, and I thank her for pushing me and motivating me to stand up for myself even when I'm scared. She taught me to love myself and to not let myself get mistreated [either] as a person [or] patient, and that is rare. That is why my nurse is so special. She is wise, funny, and most of all courageous. She is someone I hope to be moving forward in life and overall as a person, because she has impacted me to be strong even when there are many barriers against you, still fight because someone will hear you.

"Watching the emotion on each nurse's face when he/she hears their nomination story is heartwarming. The true passion of this profession is evident through each of these encounters."

Greg Opseth, BSN, RN, MHA

Funding Our Future

While Bonnie still did not believe the solution to DAISY's financial future was making hospitals pay for the award, we both knew DAISY needed help—help we could not provide or figure out ourselves. So we asked our board what to do. By our summer 2007 retreat, DAISY's board had changed considerably from our first years when it was just family and friends. Tena and Dianne were still part of it, but we now had more than a dozen nurses and other professionals advising us, including Cindy Angiulo (University of Washington), Mary Dee Hacker (Children's Hospital Los Angeles), Ann Evans (who had moved to Exempla Lutheran Medical Center in Colorado), Beth Heyman (from what was then called the Health Alliance of Greater Cincinnati), Jane Kamstra (CHRISTUS Santa Rosa), and Bonnie Lasky (University of California at San Francisco). These people traced the history of DAISY's evolution, and their relationships with us had been essential to our growth. Who better to help us chart a path forward than those who could represent the nurses we felt already owned the meaning of DAISY?

The board was united in its suggestion for whom to approach for that help: Pam Thompson, head of the American Organization of Nurse Executives (AONE), the largest professional organization for nurse leaders in the world (renamed the American Organization for Nursing Leadership or AONL in 2019). AONE could provide some insight into our business plan, administrative support, and maybe resources. We needed to ask Pam to partner DAISY and AONE.

We knew of AONE, of course. Many of the chief nursing officers and other nurse leaders with whom we worked were members, and we had been featured in its newsletter *Voice of Nursing Leadership* three years earlier. We knew the organization had marketing muscle, but we didn't need marketing. We didn't need an email blast or another article. We needed a partner. The question was: Did they? Would Pam even know who we were, and respond? There was only one way to find out. AONE had offices in Washington, DC and Chicago. Cindy said she was close to the Northwest board member, Patti Crome, and would ask her to connect us to Pam. Cindy knew Pam too, but she felt we would have a better chance of getting Pam's attention if a board member made the introduction. Cindy reached out and Patti immediately agreed to forward what we sent. Bonnie was about to write the most important email of DAISY's life.

"I will never forget writing that email," Bonnie says. "I did feel it was the most important thing I was ever going to do for DAISY, and I had one shot to do it. I went through draft after draft with Mark. We slaved over it. We thought through every word, hoping our passion for nurses would come across as strongly as we felt it. Finally we let it go."

We could only pray that Pam would respond.

❀ ❀ ❀

When Bonnie's email hit Pam's desk, she had no idea who we were. "My recognition of DAISY when Bonnie contacted me? None," says Pam. But that didn't keep her from reading what the board member had passed on: "You never know what opportunities are out there. And what DAISY had was something that we highly supported: recognizing nurses at the bedside." The human touch, the part that can't be taught from a manual like the technology and clinical side. "That's a key, important role of delivering excellent nursing care," Pam adds. "Our membership are the leaders in organizations, but they also respect the fact that the person that is at the bedside delivers the care. You can't have a good nursing department if you don't have excellence at the bedside. And so it definitely fit within one of our goals of recognizing it in a more authentic way. When Bonnie's email explained to us what she was doing, that authenticity was absolutely there. For me, DAISY represented the essence of the arts of our profession."

Pam also understood that DAISY did more than any employee-of-the-month could ever hope to do. To her, our authenticity wasn't just in the DAISY mission, but the nominations coming from the people we served—or equally as powerfully, other nurses. That sparked her interest the most. AONE had a strong commitment not only to patient-centered care but also to shared governance, defined by the American Association for Nursing Development as "a structure and process for partnership, equity, accountability, and ownership. It puts the responsibility, authority, and accountability for practice-related decisions into the hands of the individuals who will operationalize the decision."

"When DAISY reached out, AONE was working on making sure that people understood the concepts of shared governance and incorporated that into the work that they were doing," Pam recalls. "And the whole foundation of shared governance is shared leadership. What better way to recognize your colleagues then colleague to colleague? Yes there were a lot of places that were experimenting with employee engagement from the perspective of a "best employee" award and doing things like that. But they were top down. That's really important to note that. To have patients and nurses recognize it and be inspired by the care that a patient received? DAISY had all the good markings of a program that could do the right thing for nurses at the bedside in a very meaningful way. They were also very mission driven and grounded—you don't find that very often. All that intrigued me about them."

But Pam wasn't going to just offer the help of AONE sight unseen. She wanted to talk with DAISY and understand our goals and how she and AONE could help. For Pam, it was about the fit between the two, something DAISY certainly understood. It was why we made the awards both turnkey and adaptable to fit any hospital's culture. "DAISY wasn't asking for marketing," Pam notes. "Bonnie's email asked if we would be interested in helping. In order to have that conversation we needed to have a conversation. I wanted to see who these people were and have them see who we were, and make sure that there was a strong connection there."

Bonnie held her breath and clicked on the email as soon as it arrived.

"Come to Chicago. I want to meet you."

Oh my god. Oh my god. Oh my god.

❀ ❀ ❀

Since there had to be a personal connection before any partnership could be discussed, let alone fleshed out, Pam did not come alone to our meeting. She brought two of her top people: MT Meadows, the head of professional practice, and the director of operations, Sue Gergely, who later become her chief operating officer. Partnerships were not something AONE gave away easily. Partners had to jump through the hoops of a value match, mission match, and vision match first. There had been a lot of talking at AONE, and everyone thought there was something very special about what we were trying to do. We appeared to be a match. In nursing terms, we had passed the clinical test. The meeting was to ensure our human side and the story we told were as genuine in person as they seemed on paper. We were now front and center with people who would decide whether we would come into their organization or not. Pam banked on MT and Sue seeing this, and thus everyone at AONE would see what she felt: that DAISY was a wonderful way to recognize nurses that had never been put before them. If we connected in person with each of them, the rest was just details.

It was clear we all felt a connection, and Pam was right about the details. And what details! The support we got from AONE from the relationship that started that day was more than we imagined. We became for all intents and purposes part of their family, and Pam made sure they provided what we needed to thrive as a member of that family. They invited us to be a part of the annual conference, not as a vendor but as a true partner. Our booth would not be in the exhibit hall but out front at registration so every attendee would see us—something AONE had never done before. They gave us their logo to put on our nomination forms and banners. They hired a half-time assistant for us in the Chicago office who would handle inquiries and follow up on them. AONE would also start building out our new database with us, which SalesForce had donated to DAISY as a qualifying nonprofit to manage our growing number of hospitals. That work alone would be life changing for us as a business.

Anything else that needed to be done, Pam said we would figure out as the relationship developed. "I'm not a rule-bound person," Pam explains. "When you're going after something that there's no pathway established for, you make it up as you go along. DAISY had been successful for so long, if this didn't work, we would just back away and say, 'What did I learn from this?'"

Mark liked everything he heard and had just one more question for Pam that he asked that night over a martini at dinner: "What happens if we come into in a disagreement in the future?"

"We just duke it out," Pam responded.

"That sealed it for me," Mark says. "I will remember that line for the rest of my life. We use it whenever we have a disagreement, 'Let's just duke it out.'"

Shining the Light on All the Right

That future, however, came sooner than anyone thought. Bonnie and Pam started duking it out before dessert.

❋ ❋ ❋

Pam had one more thing on her mind. She looked at us across the table and bluntly addressed Bonnie's desire to keep giving DAISY as a gift: "Unless DAISY is a lot better off than it looks financially, this business model of yours has got to change. We're going to help you grow this program, but you won't be able to sustain it for long. We will bring the DAISY Award to many more hospitals than you could likely afford to fund. You have got to start charging for this program."

No one cares about nurses more than Pam, but by her own admission she can be a tough cookie. But Bonnie wasn't backing down . . . yet. "Pam, I can't do that," Bonnie said respectfully. "This is in memory of Our Patrick. I can't bring myself to do it. This is our gift to the nurses. I can't charge for it."

Bonnie looked at Pam's face as she spoke and knew immediately that if you wanted to do business with Pam, you don't say no to her without a really good business reason. And Bonnie didn't have one. Pam then politely explained why we were very wrong. She wasn't going into this recklessly. AONE's goal was to keep us running and growing long-term. She didn't have the expectation that we would stay dependent upon them. That wouldn't have been a good partnership. The value and impact DAISY provided were obviously significant. A fee would signify that value—putting their money where their mouths were, so to speak. We would bankrupt ourselves without that revenue.

"Nurse leaders will pay for the program," Pam stated confidently.

Mark was all in. He knew the value from our surveys the year before and now Pam echoed everything the hospitals said.

"Okay, we'll try," Bonnie conceded.

"Bonnie, they are going to pay for it. This is of great value. There's going to be no problem."

Bonnie wanted to believe but kept her thoughts to herself the rest of the evening. When we got home, she was still uncomfortable. She needed to be sure that Pam was right, and the only one way to do that was to talk to the chief nursing officers personally and ask them. So Bonnie called all 182 DAISY hospitals' chief nursing officers. And once again, not one of them said no. Not one thought the annual fee we agreed to with AONE—$1,250 for twelve awards per year—was unreasonable given the benefits DAISY was bringing their nurses. Every hospital went from promise to commitment as soon as the awards could be added to their budgets.

We instituted the fee in January 2008 along with our AONE partnership. That year we went from 182 to 317 hospitals. Those hospitals generated a big increase in expenses, but along with our sponsors and donors, not to mention our personal contributions, DAISY generated enough in income to cover it. We were not just going to survive as a business—we were going to thrive. AONE provided the guidance of nursing leadership to make our vision a sustainable reality. Pam Thompson believed the mark of our success would be that we could go and hire our own staff. That we then could go partner with as many other people and organizations as we wanted and grow it beyond our imagination.

We are often asked by other nursing organizations that support our mission why AONE (now AONL) gets to have their logo on our banner and honoree certificate. To us the reason is clear: They were the first. Their guidance was invaluable. We wouldn't be here without them. Pam saw what we were doing as universal, because nursing is universal. "You'll find that art, that essence, no matter where you find nurses," she says. "My privilege of meeting so many nurses internationally is that once you get down to that essence, all the other stuff doesn't matter. We have different governments, we have different health systems, but we all take care of patients and families. It's not about your technology. It's not about who or what has got the best systems. It has nothing to do with any of that. It's: Do you have nurses that understand how to deliver care at that level? That's what we do. That's what DAISY could help us do."

And we did. Because of AONE and Pam. Because of the *nurses*. All we wanted to do was thank you, and ten years later look what they did!

Everything DAISY was about to change for the better.

DAISY HONOREE STORY

Wesley Runnels, RN, BSN, CCRN

Thomas Hospital
Fairhope, Alabama

The 22-year Army veteran and author John Holmes wrote: "There is no exercise better for the heart than reaching down and lifting people up." In the Cardiac Intensive Care Unit, Wes Runnels went above and beyond to continuously and compassionately offer a healing hand to lift the spirits of my Army veteran and me after his heart surgery. This nurse's demonstration of compassion made a special connection with us. We feel compelled to say thank you for how much we appreciate Wes's care and skill during W's critical ICU stay at Thomas Hospital.

The surgery was risky simply because of his age, but necessary to have any chance to maintain his quality of life. I will never forget as they wheeled him away and down the corridor to surgery, his hand went up with one last wave.

My heart cinched at the thought of the hand I knew so well possibly waving goodbye. That was the hand I held as he said "I do." One hand of a pair that had worked, carved, built our home, and carried our children and grandchildren.

The surgery was over. Success! My W was in recovery, and I could see him. Thirty minutes passed. Then an hour went by. Each time the phone rang, I would jump, hoping it was for me. Slowly, evening arrived, and other families saw their loved ones and left for the day. I was the last one in the ICU waiting room, so when the phone rang, I expected to see W finally.

Nearly ten hours after my husband waved when wheeled off to surgery, a nurse named Wes entered our lives. He immediately seemed to identify that I was scared and shut down, my hands tied. He saw how my mind and fears had begun to take root and overwhelm me. He sat beside me and spoke calmly and clearly, explaining that the doctor had made the best choice for my W. He explained in a way I could understand that blood had pooled around his heart.

I had allowed my mind to grow uneasy, and my heart had sunk, but Wes reached down and lifted me back up. My emotions had run so high that my brain could not process facts before Wes took matters into his own hands. He had patience and used a relatable vernacular. At that moment, I felt God blessed Wes with extraordinary nursing skills and compassion for his patient's family, and He also answered my prayers.

Wes never made us feel like we asked "silly" questions or were "old people" who inconvenienced him. He welcomed every need and every question with the utmost interest and concern. Wes made my husband and me both feel like we mattered. In the most professional way possible, it was clear that Wes cared about his responsibility as a nurse and about my husband's recovery.

Wes was the night nurse, but he was the light during our arduous and dark stay in the ICU.

Growing DAISY
2008–2019

"The DAISY Award is very special because it is not about my degree
or academic achievements. The award is about how I care for
my patients and shows that my patient's family and my
coworkers see how much I love to care for others."

Christine Duerksen, RN

What's a Nice Girl Like You . . .

Saudi Arabia, 2015. Bonnie was wandering the desert. Mark was sure of it. She had been gone 10 minutes in the pitch-black night surrounding their campsite in the vast sands surrounding Jeddah. Maybe in the story of Exodus, her people had wandered the desert for 40 years on their journey to the Promised Land. But Bonnie's a nice Jewish girl from New York City. She wasn't looking for the land of milk and honey, just the only tree nearby to pee behind. She had initially refused to go but necessity overcame her modesty. Mark pointed the way and out she went, iPhone with no cellular reception lighting the way. The tree wasn't far. Ten minutes was too long to be gone. So Mark stood outside the tent, called out for Bonnie, and a light suddenly appeared, a hundred yards away, headed in the wrong direction. She quickly turned around.

Ironically, Bonnie was only lost that night because by 2015 DAISY had been found and embraced by thousands of hospitals worldwide, including seven in Saudi Arabia (rising to 21 by our 20th anniversary). It's not lost on us that when we started DAISY we had been wandering too—maybe not in a desert but certainly unsure of exactly where we were going and how long it would take to get there. Not anymore. DAISY had started to cover the world like the sand that covered us the next morning after a sandstorm hit during the night.

How did we get here? Nurses, of course. Their compassionate care DAISY recognizes knows no borders.

❁ ❁ ❁

Our 2015 trip wasn't our first to Saudi Arabia, though it was our first time camping there. Our hosts, King Faisal Specialist Hospital and Research Centre 's chief nursing officer Sandy Lovering and her husband, Craig, had piled us, tons of equipment, and extra tires into their Range Rover for a night. As we drove out of Jeddah, we don't know what fascinated us more: the baboons on the side of the road or the fact that there was a Cinnabon in the gas station we stopped at on the outskirts of the city. When we returned to Jeddah after a night at our magnificent campsite, we addressed the 7th International Nursing Symposium on Embracing Magnet in the Middle East.

Our first introduction to Saudi Arabia was in 2009 when we attended our first Magnet conference in the United States organized by the American Nurses Credentialing Center (ANCC). Magnet is the designation given by the ANCC to hospitals that excel in quality care delivered by nurses and their organizations. Earlier in the year, ANCC's executive director, Jeanne Floyd, had sent us a letter saying she had

Camels and cars in the Saudi desert, 2015

become aware of our work. She hoped we would have time to talk with her about how ANCC could be helpful toward supporting the DAISY Award in every Magnet hospital—and eventually the organization's Pathway to Excellence program, which it was then in the process of acquiring. *Would we have time? Are you kidding us?* We were so excited you'd have thought DAISY had been designated Magnet!

To start, ANCC invited us to do what AONE did: set up our display outside the exhibit hall as a partner, not with the vendors. We put together a homemade booth, and that's where we were when we met Judy Moseley, who told us she'd like to bring DAISY to the hospital where she was chief nursing officer: King Faisal Specialist Hospital and Research Centre in Riyadh, Saudi Arabia. *You want to do what where?* Judy is a tall, blonde, stately woman who that day was dressed in a stylish, light pantsuit—hardly the match for what we pictured a Saudi nurse might look like. "I'm from Minneapolis," she explained, adding that most of the nurses at her hospital and throughout Saudi Arabia were expats. Nursing is not as respected a profession there as it is in the U.S. Judy wanted her staff to feel part of the global community of nurses and feel the pride of being honored with DAISY.

Our discussion with Judy tapped into our already growing excitement being at an international conference. We didn't know much about nursing in other countries, and our relationship with ANCC and presence at the Magnet conference was bound to bring even more international inquiries. This was all something new for us to consider as we grew. Thanks to our AONE relationship, DAISY was adding more than 100 hospitals a year and we projected close to 500 total by the end of 2009. But we had only one international hospital and it wasn't all that foreign: The Hospital for Sick Children in Toronto. Bonnie had been thinking about approaching one of the nursing organizations in Canada to do what AONE had done for us here. But did we want to expand overseas? Serving Canada didn't seem like it should be that much harder or different from serving the States.

Was DAISY just about American nursing? Would honoring nurses internationally distract us from our growth at home—growth we had just started to manage now that hospitals were paying?

In the end, we decided DAISY was about honoring the compassionate care of nurses anywhere they are, and King Faisal Specialist Hospital and Research Centre in Riyadh became our first hospital outside of North America, quickly followed by King Faisal in Jeddah and the American University Medical Center in Beirut. By the end of 2010, we had six international partners. But it wasn't until 2012 when Donna Hilliard, director of nursing education at King Fahad Medical City in Riyadh, invited us to speak at an international nursing symposium that we understood firsthand the global connection between nurses and DAISY—and that nurses are nurses everywhere.

Getting to talk to nurses in Saudi Arabia was a big deal! To meet those nurses in Saudi Arabia, however, Bonnie needed to dress appropriately. Our friend and DAISY Nurse Deidre Stewart bought her a long black abaya so she would be covered neck to toe and a chiffon *shayla* (scarf) to cover her hair (she was not required to cover half her face with a veil). She put them on before we landed in Riyadh and even found the abaya really comfortable when she wasn't tripping on its length. As a man, Mark had no such restrictions on his dress but would happily have dressed any way they wanted for a glass of wine with dinner; the Saudi ban on alcohol had started on the plane.

Donna greeted us at the airport wearing a lab coat and a shayla similar to Bonnie's, her outfit almost the entire time we were with her. After 18 years in Saudi Arabia, Donna and many of the other expat nurses were adept at navigating and explaining the "Saudi way." When we spotted all the logos of American fast-food chains on our drive from the hotel—McDonald's, KFC, Taco Bell, the names all written in Arabic—Donna told us the country didn't have an obesity problem until those chains came to town. When we spotted several Starbucks, Donna told us women are not welcome to sit in the same area as men. In the hospital, she showed us separate waiting and prayer rooms for men only. How do female nurses treat patients of the opposite sex? More jarring was seeing all the Saudi women—nurses and patients—in

Nurses welcoming us at King Faisal Specialist Hospital and Research Centre in Jeddah, 2015

the hospital dressed in abayas and shaylas with black veils that left only their eyes showing. How do they deal with the abayas for IVs?

We had all our questions answered, because underneath the dress the nurses were the same welcoming, informative, gracious, proud, and of course compassionate people we knew in the States. They talked with us about the clinical and compassionate challenges of being a nurse in Saudi Arabia. We are told that families are obligated by Islam to visit their patients, and as many as 15 people might be in a room at any time. Sometimes they bring in food and lay it out on blankets on the floor. The nurses have a tough time dealing with this just to control infection, but family and spiritual requirements are heeded first and foremost. Because that's where compassion has its origin in an Islamic hospital, and they put the needs of the patient first. Donna and her colleagues told us they hoped DAISY would soon come to King Fahad Medical City.

We would soon know how likely that was, because before we spoke at the conference, the hospital's chief nursing officer, Jane Wilshaw, had arranged for a meeting with King Fahad Medical City's CEO, Abdullah Al Amro. Jane had shared the abstract of our talk with him ("The Power of Gratitude: Driving Patient- and Family-Centered Care with Nurse Recognition"), and he asked to meet with us and the nurses to discuss DAISY. While waiting in his sitting room outside his office, two men in black suits brought us dates and cardamom coffee, and we realized we did not know what to expect. We had been given very specific instructions from dress to decorum, like don't touch him unless he reaches out to you. We did not know if Bonnie would be permitted to speak. The nurses around us fidgeted nervously.

As soon as we were ushered in, a tall, slender, bearded man wearing the traditional Arabic dress we had only seen on sheiks in pictures and on TV greeted us. He sat in a big chair and motioned at the sofa next to him for us to sit. He leaned in and said, "Tell me your story." With those words, Dr. Al Amro completely disarmed us and listened intently as we told him the story of DAISY. He told us his story too, covering his training in Canada, his family, his work as a doctor, his recent recognition as CEO of the year, his upcoming trip to Korea to speak, and his eagerness to step down from his marathon job. He then told us he had great regard for nurses and was totally supportive of DAISY being part of King Fahad Medical City. He was excited to kick off the program with us.

We spent 20 minutes together before we headed down to the auditorium to speak. Dr. Al Amro gave the opening speech on the history of nursing in the Arab world, going all the way back to Maimonides. He then invited us on stage to receive a gift from him. Bonnie still didn't know whether to shake his hand or not. (When Bonnie got on the elevator to head to the auditorium, the men backed away from her.) But he immediately put his hand out to shake hers. Much to Mark's chagrin, Bonnie still has a crush on him.

❀ ❀ ❀

Our meetings with the nurses and Dr. Al Amro showed us the universal power of recognition and gratitude. Even in a country where nurses did not command universal respect, and regardless of any cultural differences between our countries, DAISY has been warmly welcomed. Today, our signs are in Arabic and numerous other languages including Mandarin (although our daisy in China is red, as white is the color of death). We have circled the globe several times over to visit many of the countries DAISY is in and have been greeted in ways we will never forget. In São Paulo, Brazil, nurses at the Hospital Israelita Albert Einstein seemed to take every daisy in South America to create a floor-to-ceiling curtain of daisies as a backdrop for our visit. At Bumrungrad International Hospital in Bangkok, we were shown by the CEO how every DAISY Nurse receives a gorgeous banner with their nomination story written on it. At Nottingham University Hospitals NHS Trust in England, the nurse leaders had a DAISY tea for us dressed up in vintage nursing outfits, displaying the history of their uniforms through the years. The tables were set with their personal tea sets. The chief nurse at England's Northampton General Hospital even goes on local radio asking for patients to nominate nurses.

And then there is Vietnam. We are there because of one man: Greg Crow, a nurse who tragically passed away in 2019. Greg had

Riley Barnes Carraher and Peter Maher joined Bonnie and Mark at the dedication of the DAISY Wall at Nottingham University Hospitals NHS Trust in England, 2018. The nurses dressed in vintage nursing outfits.

been a professor at the University of San Francisco and had become a consultant to hospitals on shared governance. We heard him speak at an event at San Francisco General Hospital where he was given its Friend of Nursing Award, an honor DAISY had received a year earlier. Greg detailed his volunteer work in Vietnam, a country he loved. He described how he educated nurses through a program called the Vietnam Nurses Project, in which he took nurse educators from San Francisco and beyond to work with the Vietnamese nurses on clinical care. We met him briefly after the event and asked if he knew about the DAISY Award. He did and told us that he would love to bring it to Vietnam. Sure enough, a couple of years later he called and said, "I'm going to Vietnam, and I'm bringing DAISY with me. Do you want to come?" We shipped a big box of everything needed and tagged along with him for the first DAISY ceremony.

When we say nurses are nurses everywhere in the world, this trip exemplified it. It doesn't matter how broad or limited their scope of practice is. They still have that human heart that beats at the center of DAISY and owns the program no matter what language they speak. But we had never seen conditions like the ones in the first hospital we visited in Vietnam. Their intensive care unit was a twelve-bed ward. There were no individual rooms. Family members helped patients in the ICU. There was a washing machine in the back and sheets hanging by the windows to dry. The nurses in Saudi Arabia had every resource imaginable. The nurses here lacked basic items like stethoscopes, and seemed pleased to have running water. (The government hospital we visited later that trip had the best of the best, but not this one.) And yet the nurses there were just as heartbreakingly wonderful, conscientious, and compassionate as those in Saudi Arabia and in the most modern and technologically advanced hospitals in the United States we knew. Part of the goal of the Vietnam Nurses Project would be to use DAISY to upgrade the level of acceptance and recognition of nurses in the country.

As of 2019, DAISY honors nurses in more than 150 hospitals in 25 countries outside the United States. In addition to our work with the American Nurses Credentialing Center, our partnerships with the International Council of Nursing and Sigma Theta Tau International help us reach nurses worldwide.

But we have gotten ahead of ourselves in this story, because while we have done most of the international visits, we no longer oversee the international hospitals day-to-day. They are served at DAISY by a woman who joined us in 2011 and was used to opening a Starbucks store she managed at 3:00 A.M.—and thus never minds being up early to do international webinars: Melissa Barnes, one of our daughters-in-law. In our second decade, DAISY had become a family business, starting with the person who shared the memory of Our Patrick with us the most.

DAISY HONOREE STORY

Gill Gull, RN
University Hospitals of Leicester
Leicester, United Kingdom

Being admitted for heart surgery had to be one of the scariest times of my life. As a resilient person both personally and professionally, this was completely challenging as I found myself feeling both vulnerable and emotional. Tears would flow freely for no reason as I struggled to comprehend all I had been through.

Until Gill came along!

She oozed compassion and kindness. She would listen to me, sit with me, and recognize my distress. She knew she couldn't fix it, but made me feel cared for and safe so that I could cry and express how I felt. As a nurse [myself], I can only describe Gill as a phenomenal nurse who made me feel stronger emotionally each day. Gill's empathy and kindness have made a huge impact on me and my recovery. There are no words to describe how she's made me feel. She is one very special nurse who sprinkles fairy dust everywhere she goes.

"I cannot tell you how incredibly special this DAISY Award has been to me. It may sound crazy but having received this award has made me a better nurse. The sense of pride that I feel when people that I barely know come up to congratulate me and tell me that no one deserves it more, it brings tears to my eyes each time."

Donna Young, RN

We Are Family

"How are you going to manage three young kids and do school full time?"

Tena looked at Bonnie, tears welling in her eyes as she answered. "I don't know and quite frankly I'm terrified."

It was just before Christmas of 2009, and we were visiting Tena and Riley in Atlanta for the holiday and Tena's birthday. Bonnie and Tena were doing the dishes while the rest of the family made noise in the dining room. Tena had remarried in the years after Patrick died, to a lovely man named John Carraher, and they'd had two children together, Lauren and Kate. She had been raising all three kids while we were raising DAISY. She was also working for the advertising company where she and Patrick had met in Atlanta. But now Tena wanted to build a new career as . . . a nurse! She had been accepted at a local nursing college and was to start after the holidays.

Tena's decision to become a nurse wasn't entirely because of DAISY. She was not involved in our day-to-day operations, though she had been on our board from the beginning and attended every meeting. She went to local DAISY events too, and had even introduced the awards to Piedmont Hospital in downtown Atlanta after Lauren was born and had to spend some time in the NICU. Initially being involved in anything public for DAISY was difficult for Tena. She loved John deeply, but the memory of losing Patrick still made her emotional. We saw this firsthand when we came in for the inaugural DAISY Award at Piedmont. "As I stepped forward to present I thought, *I've got this. I can do this*," Tena recalls. "I think I squeaked out three words and the tears came and I just took a couple steps back. Mark and Bonnie stepped forward and I said, 'Okay, maybe I'm not ready to be on my own yet.'"

Since then, Tena has learned to "turn her feelings upside down" for the most part and smiles at all that DAISY is doing in Pat's memory, remembering their happy times together and focusing on the nurses. And of course there was Riley. DAISY connected Riley to the memory of the father she never got to know. Tena brought her to every board meeting, and she attended other events, too. It wasn't *that* hard to get her to go. Like father, like daughter: Riley would go anywhere for a Cinnabon. But she also loved the nurses, and the nurses loved when she came to events with Tena or us, especially when we visited Riley Children's Hospital in Indiana. In 2011, Riley participated in the 10th anniversary celebration of our first award at the University of Washington. In 2012, she asked to go on our three-week drive to visit hospitals in the Midwest.

But it wasn't Riley's or her connection to DAISY that pushed Tena to want a career in nursing. It was a nurse she met at Piedmont who told her she had lost her son to leukemia at age nine. "I decided to be a nurse to give back to the nurses who took care of him." Tena thought, *This is what I want to do. I've met so many nurses who have made such a difference and this could be a way that I can give back.* So she went back to school to do the math and science prerequisites she needed in addition to her bachelor's degree, and she was finally ready to start nursing school in January 2010. But just taking the time to complete those prerequisites had been stressful. Tena said her family was "pretty much on strike because all I did was study or go to class." Bonnie knew this, which was why she asked the question about how she would manage.

Not because we wanted to pry, but because we had another question ready.

"This is probably bad timing, but we're growing," Bonnie said. "We really need someone to work full-time for the foundation. Why don't you come work for DAISY and not go to nursing school?"

Tena looked at Bonnie and asked wryly, "Why didn't you discuss this with me two years ago when I was starting my prerequisites?!"

"Because we didn't know we would need you," Bonnie replied. DAISY was now adding well over 200 hospitals a year and projected to reach 1,000 hospitals by 2012. One part-time person from AONE was not nearly enough to get the work done. "I'm drowning and need help."

Our vision was Tena would be the point of contact in the East, Bonnie in the West, and Mark would handle the finances and shipping with the help of John Reynolds. Tena said she needed to talk to her husband and think about it. She promised an answer before we left. We understood why and did not take it personally. She had worked hard to get into nursing school and had been looking forward to becoming a nurse. But she soon realized DAISY was her first labor of love, and the possibility of honoring so many nurses would allow her to impact more people than she ever imagined.

Tena accepted our job offer two days later, and we all started hugging and crying. That's when Lauren came in and said, "Mommy, does this mean that you're a nurse now?"

"No," Tena answered, "but I'm going to be working with nurses."

"Okay."

And then Lauren joined the hugging and crying as well.

❁ ❁ ❁

Truth be told, we needed Tena for more than just the work. We needed someone who understood DAISY. Who felt a connection to it and the nurses. Who understood its mission. Who would love it. No one could have a closer connection to the origin story of DAISY than she did, but she also understood why DAISY was different from any other recognition program. She got the importance of it not coming from within the hospital. Plus her desire to be a nurse gave her added respect for them and their ability to manage work, life, continuing education, and family and be as she says "multitasking, high achieving, amazing humans."

"I hear a lot of nurses say, 'DAISY came when I needed it the most' or 'This award made me feel like I made a difference' or 'It means so much that someone took the time to do this for me.'" Tena says. "In this day and age, I think a lot of people will take the time to write a complaint. We wanted patients and families to tell their stories and thank their nurses for making a positive impact. I think that so many people do it speaks volumes about the profession and for DAISY as well. When we're visiting hospitals or at conferences, nurses come up and want to personally thank us. They want to hug us, take pictures with us. They cry when they explain what it meant to them to be nominated for and receive the DAISY Award. One nurse came up to me and said she had been a nurse for 52 years and pointed at her nominee pin. 'This was from a patient. It was one of the highlights of my career.' She just wanted to say thank you to us, but our mission was to say thank you to people like her. And now they 'owned' the program!"

Tena got it for sure, but with DAISY growing so rapidly we soon needed more help—a lot more help. Mark could not possibly handle the finances, order everything that went with the awards, and do most of the shipping, along with everything else he was doing. Bonnie needed more than just Tena to support the organizational work. We needed someone who understood standardization *and* that everything we do is about supporting the nurses, helping them execute the program, and educating them on how to take best advantage of it. We needed another person who would love DAISY.

Lucky for us, we had another daughter-in-law who was expert in all that we needed to help transform DAISY operationally: Auntie Bonkers.

* * *

Auntie Bonkers is Riley's nickname for Melissa Barnes, Patrick's brother Adam's wife, who lives in Seattle. The nickname belies her professional skill but not her personality. In 2011, Melissa was managing a large and successful Starbucks. We were having breakfast with her one morning and started pumping her for information on how Starbucks makes sure everything is done the same way and remains true to the values of the brand. She knew why we were asking and shifted the conversation to us and DAISY and what we could be doing.

The two of us had the same thought: *Melissa should be working for DAISY.* "What are you doing at Starbucks? You should be working for DAISY! You can see your kids in the morning. If you come work for us, you can have a life!"

Melissa smiled, "I've been waiting for you to ask me."

We knew Melissa, like Tena, would succeed not just because she was smart and a good worker, but because she also loved DAISY and the nurses we served. "Having married Patrick's brother and seeing what Bonnie and Mark were doing—the excitement whenever they made a partnership with a new hospital. Watching it grow and grow and grow and seeing everything they got to do. They got to share gratitude with nurses. I don't think you're going to find very many people that say, 'I get to work for my in-laws and enjoy it.' I wanted to be part of what they created for the better of nursing and the world. I wanted to be part of the journey and had promised to be there when they needed me. I had a great job, but this was the right job for me," Melissa recalls.

At first Melissa took over the western United States from Bonnie in 2011 and then dove into our systems. We had a plan for communicating with hospitals, and we had SalesForce up and running fairly well. We were handling billing and shipping. We had a "welcome kit" for every new hospital we signed up that included a binder explaining chapter and verse of how to run the program. The problem was, we were not as systematic as we wanted to be. DAISY didn't feel scalable. Melissa's operational skills and experience were perfect for us. She would set up the standards that would make us better at serving our "customers" as we continued to grow.

Melissa's goal was to continually find what worked really well, get feedback from us and Tena on what we needed, and then take that and figure out a way to share it with everyone who had the program. To do this, she took the time to understand why some programs got so much out of DAISY, and she used that to create a set of best practices that we shared with all the hospitals via webinars. She used her business and buying background to create an operations plan so every new organization was trained on how to implement DAISY from the moment they signed up. Everything our partners needed to do to be successful was included, and they were trained in how to do it all: building a selection committee, attracting nominations, tracking and blinding nominations, building awareness with marketing and PR, using the materials and templates we provided for nomination forms and award certificates, scheduling and presenting awards, and ordering more.

Tena worked with Melissa to revamp our welcome kit and connect it more effectively to a new password-protected Resource Center on our website. Melissa then worked with all of us to adapt SalesForce into what we needed to capture everything from communications history to stories. To handle all this, Melissa used her human resources experience to hire her own team, initially a few people she had managed at Starbucks, growing to DAISY's current team of 15 based in their home offices all over the United States. And when we put more energy behind our international growth, Melissa's comfort getting up in the middle of the night to open her Starbucks store, combined with her interest in foreign culture, made her an easy fit to oversee DAISY's growing international footprint, too.

❊ ❊ ❊

With Tena, Melissa, and our growing regional staff on board, we started to see how we could step back from the day-to-day work as

Ten years later we're still family: Melissa, Tena, Bonnie, and Mark, 2019. Photo by Kenneth Krehbiel, Imageworks Photography.

the organization grew, focusing our efforts on strategic planning and DAISY's visibility to the nursing profession. They gave us the expertise and bandwidth to ensure that DAISY delivered on our commitment to the nurses and hospitals since the liquid dinner: that the program would be turnkey. We would guide its implementation with the hospitals, and they could customize it to their size and culture.

But most importantly with Tena and Melissa, we had and were building a staff that feels like our family. Mark was finally getting what he wanted: DAISY was running like a family *and* a business. Everyone knew that Our Patrick was the reason DAISY existed and that everything reminded nurses how special they are. Melissa's systems were making everything run more efficiently. In other words, our standards reflected the equivalent of compassionate care and clinical excellence— the standards nurses hold themselves to every day.

Our board, now filled with chief nursing officers and leaders in the healthcare industry, ensured this as well, as did the man who would become our chief financial officer, Peter Maher. Peter came from Mark's second family: the advertising business he had sold years before DAISY. Peter had risen from staff accountant to chief financial officer under Mark, and there was no one Mark trusted more with money. Peter had left the business shortly after Mark did and started his own financial consulting company. So when DAISY was growing, Mark constantly called him with accounting questions. Peter soon started volunteering his time doing what he called the "bits and pieces" to help us, refusing to take any money. But what started with him setting up a simple accounting system soon became more complex work. More than half of Peter's consulting work is now for DAISY, so we offered and he begrudgingly accepted a small pittance for his time. In 2010, we asked Peter to join our board and assume the title of chief financial officer, which he has been ever since.

But Peter's love for DAISY is not because of his close friendship to Mark. Given the opportunity, Mark will tell the tale of Peter proving his disloyalty to him when he happened to be in attendance for one of our aggressive discussions. As Mark recalls, Peter immediately took Bonnie's side: "This was a man I had placed all my trust in. A man I personally raised through the ranks of my previous company, as well as DAISY. And then when an opportunity to support me in my hour of need presented itself, he chose to rush to the other side. I now call him by one name: Benedict." Ah, family.

What binds ~~Benedict~~ Peter to DAISY is what binds us all: the nurses. Peter has made exactly one demand of us since he started: to attend the annual Magnet conference with us so he can be with the nurses. He hangs out at our booth and talks to nurses. He takes pictures with them. He takes pictures of us with them. He asks them to tell their stories. He thanks them. You see, Peter had open heart surgery in 2009 after other procedures failed to make him better. (He was only in his forties but has a family history of heart disease.) He never forgot what the nurses meant to him during the entire process, and the comfort they gave him as he recovered.

Because everyone has a nurse story, and to serve those nurses and their stories, the DAISY Awards were about to expand their reach.

DAISY HONOREE STORY

Quinn C. Jackson, BSN, RN
Providence St. Vincent Medical Center
Portland. Oregon

I recently had back surgery. The procedure was longer and more involved than anticipated. After surgery, I was taken to recovery until my pain was under control, then I could be taken to my room. I am 83 years old, and embarrassed to say I was in so much pain, I just yelled out with every movement or touch. I was given an attendant nurse and he was very soft-spoken and gentle (despite all my noise!). He told me I was maxing out pain meds, but he wanted to know if he could step away for a few minutes. He came back with his guitar and asked if it was okay if he played for me. Then he sang two songs very softly while he played. It did not remove the pain, but my head became very much at ease. I got teary at his kindness and voice.

Later, when I told my family about this, they too were moved by this gesture. I don't know if St. Vincent's uses such things to help patients cope (or to quiet them down!), but I want to think this man did it "just for me" when I needed it! All the nurses and staff were wonderful, but I will never forget this special act of kindness! Thank you.

"Being a DAISY Team Award winner is such a humbling experience. This award recognized all our team for a job well done. I'm so proud of all of our nurses and the true difference they make each and every day!"

Meredith Hartzog, BSN, RN, CVRN-BC

What Happened to Turnkey?!

When we conceived of the DAISY Awards, one of our objectives was to create a turnkey operation. And it was. It consisted of an award pin, a certificate in a Costco frame (later a professional portfolio), a box of Cinnabons, a massage, dinner, and (a year into the program) the *Healer's Touch* sculpture. Very simple. Very turnkey. Then, as Mark says, "Nurses really screwed that up."

First came their inspiration for the addition of a banner. *That's terrific, let's steal, um, share that idea with everyone else.* Then came a nominee pin. *Love that—let's make them for everyone!* Then they opened our eyes to the fact that the massage and dinner were unimportant—that DAISY is about the recognition. *Wonderful, we don't want to give nurses something that isn't important to them!* How about that great DAISY Committee button: Ask Me About the DAISY Award? *We need that, too! Let's order them.* Then the multiple nominee pin. *Really?! Another great addition!*

Every time we caught up to nurses' ideas, they came up with a new one. In other words, nurses kept making the DAISY Awards better. But if we thought nurses would stop there, we were sadly mistaken. They then made the DAISY Awards bigger, not just better.

❀ ❀ ❀

Actually, the first time a nurse caused us to expand DAISY wasn't for the awards but for the foundation itself, and connected to one of our ideas from the liquid dinner in 1999 with Tena and Dianne that started it all: funding research in treatment of patients with autoimmune diseases like ITP. We had given up the research dream once we realized we didn't have the money to make a difference. But even as we grew, we wanted research to be part of the DAISY mission somehow. We mentioned this at the 2007 DAISY board meeting, hoping our advisors would have thoughts on how we could raise funds for it and where the money might go.

Cindy Angiulo, assistant administrator for the University of Washington Medical Center who had made it her charge to put our first DAISY Awards together in 2001, had an idea. "If you are so interested in research," she said, looking around the table, "then why not marry your passion for nurses' care for patients with your desire to fund research for patient care by starting a grant program for nursing research?"

We'll be candid: When Cindy proposed this, we were stunned. We looked at each other, and Bonnie blurted out what Mark was also thinking, "Nurses do *research*?"

We had no idea of the level of science being applied by nurses to patient care through thoughtful, structured research studies. And we didn't really understand what evidence-based practice projects were or how they differed from research studies. It was a huge epiphany and suffice it to say, Cindy and the other nurses on the board gave us a thorough education. When they were done, we had the foundation for the launch of the J. Patrick Barnes Grants for Nursing Research and Evidence-Based Practice Projects.

Since Patrick had cancer as a young man and then ITP, we decided to focus on providing grants for nursing research and evidence-based projects designed to improve care for patients with one of those two conditions. To ensure the projects connected to DAISY's dedication to nurses and their direct care of patients, we made one of the requirements that staff nurses have to be deeply engaged in every study. For example, if a proposal involved surveys, nurse-researchers needed to have staff nurses analyze those surveys, not simply hand them out and log the answers. By nurturing this culture of inquiry among nurses, DAISY would also play a role in ensuring patients stayed at the heart of evidence-based healthcare.

Cindy agreed to chair the program and asked Elizabeth Bridges, a world-renowned researcher and critical care nurse, to build a volunteer panel of nurse-scientists to review applications. Liz loved the idea, especially about engaging staff nurses in research. The DAISY grant program just took off from there. By 2019, we had committed approximately $500,000 to hundreds of nurses' projects. Today, the program is run by a panel of 13 nurse-scientists. The panelists make sure that the projects we fund are well thought out and good science. To help our grantees disseminate their findings throughout the world of patient care, we added the Lynne Doll Grants for Dissemination of Findings in memory of our dear, departed board member and friend. Those grants provide funding for nurses to present their work at nursing conferences, and can be used for things like poster production, conference fees, and travel. In addition, in 2019, after we kept getting calls from nurses about asking for funding for the medical missions they were going on, we added the DAISY Medical Mission Grants, for DAISY to help pay for their participation in missions that allow them to share their compassion and skill with nurses and patients in underserved areas.

❀ ❀ ❀

With the grant program now in place, nurses turned their attention to the reach and mission of the awards themselves and whom they went to, because more nurses than we ever imagined wanted to be DAISY Nurses. Consider these words a nurse manager said to us during her hospital's award celebration: "I love DAISY and that my nurses are getting this kind of recognition. They really deserve it for all they do at the bedside. But I'll never be a DAISY! I'm not eligible because I'm not doing much direct care anymore."

We're not identifying that nurse by name, because she was not unique. In talking to nurse managers and directors, we heard a similar refrain and took it to heart. In addition, more and more organizations wanted to recognize their nurse leaders in a meaningful way. After all, nurse leaders have a tremendous impact on patient care and the environments where the compassion DAISY recognizes is going on. We wouldn't have had great nurses at Patrick's bedside if they hadn't had leaders empowering and supporting them. And many nurse leaders do hands-on work with patients.

So we created the DAISY Nurse Leader Award to express gratitude for courageous and caring nurse leaders who inspire compassion and create environments in which it can thrive. Nurse leaders who listen. Who help their nurses find the extraordinary in everyday acts of kindness. Who recognize the power nurses have to touch others. We launched the DAISY Nurse Leader Award at the 2015 AONE Annual Meeting and recognized the first recipients later that year. Over time, participating DAISY organizations have used this award to recognize lots of nursing roles such as preceptors, educators, charge nurses, and informaticists who have an indirect impact on patient care.

Okay, fine, the DAISY Nurse Leader Award was the one new award that we initiated, but it was still inspired by nurses who compelled us to screw up our turnkey operation ourselves. Not so the DAISY Team Award, which had arrived a couple of years before.

❀ ❀ ❀

Of course, celebrating teamwork was one of the reasons that we asked that Patrick's gift to his nurses—Cinnabon cinnamon rolls—be shared with everyone in the DAISY Honorees' units. Because that's what Patrick wanted when we brought him Cinnabons in the hospital. DAISY Nurses constantly reminded us that they could not do what they do without their teams. But it took a phone call in 2013 from Rachel Behrendt, a nurse leader and at the time our key contact at Thomas Jefferson University Hospital in Philadelphia, to get us to add teams to the DAISY Award roster. She told us about all the DAISY Award nominations Thomas Jefferson was receiving for teams doing extraordinary things for patients and their families who couldn't name a specific person who did something more spectacular than another.

DAISY Team Award to the Surgical Care Unit at Children's National Medical Center, Washington, DC, 2017

"I need to create a team award. How would you feel about a team award?" she asked.

"Are the teams made up of all nurses?"

"Not always."

"Are they nurse led?"

"Yes. Always."

"Then let's do it."

Thus the DAISY Team Award was created with Rachel piloting the first one. And we are so glad it was. It has been a great addition to our statement of gratitude to nurses. Over the years we have heard many Team Award stories about baptisms, graduations, weddings, special outings, end-of-life celebrations . . . But none touched us more than when we presented the award to the nurses and staff at Adventist Feather River Hospital in Paradise, California.

Paradise is the town that was destroyed in the horrific Camp Fire of 2018. As the town burned, more than 40 Adventist Health Feather River nurses and staff remained to evacuate the hospital. *As their own homes were on fire and they were thinking they would never see their families again, their first duty was to their patients.* Think about that. For a time, these people did not think they would survive, let alone be able to help their patients. Yet these heroes managed to evacuate 62 patients—some just out of surgery, some just born—in 45 minutes. We had the privilege of personally presenting the DAISY Team Award to them in 2018, and it was among the most moving moments in our entire DAISY journey. Their stories were harrowing, their courage and strength impossible to fully capture in words and almost unbelievable. It was truly a miracle they all survived and can tell their chilling stories today. (You can watch a video that captures some of those stories on YouTube. Just search for "Angels in Paradise.")

The near-instant acceptance of the DAISY Team Award by the nurses was no doubt also due, in part, to the increased emphasis in healthcare on building interprofessional teams. As a result, it allowed doctors—who are also not eligible for DAISY Awards but often long to be—to be recognized as part of the teams they value being a part of. One chief of staff at a hospital was so eager to be recognized by DAISY, he kept poking his head into our event there, filling our water glasses, and asking us if doing this would allow us to "make him a DAISY." We told him that's not how it works, but if he was on a nurse-led team, then he would get the recognition he longed for along with the nurses and staff.

Mary Dee Hacker, formerly the chief nursing officer at Children's Hospital Los Angeles and a member of our board, sums up the power of the Team Award perfectly: "DAISY Nurses love being DAISY Nurses. The Team Award is a cherished and appreciated recognition that extends DAISY's reach. It's amazing to me to see that people who are the most excited about receiving the award are the physicians who love the feeling of recognition and gratitude. Like the nurses, they choose their profession for a lot of reasons but primarily because they want to make a difference. They want to do something that matters. So much of the environment in healthcare is about productivity standards and outcome measurements. To pause for a few minutes and hear someone say, 'We want to thank you for your heart' really matters."

The irony is that the emphasis in healthcare on interprofessional teams is the number one reason some hospitals do not have the DAISY Awards at all: Some don't want to honor nurses separately. They think it undermines morale to have a recognition program that focuses on nurses as a separate entity and want to have the same award for all their disciplines. Okay, but in the end a single standardized recognition program for all employees could never do what DAISY does for nurses. Nurses have a unique connection to a hospital's customers: the patients. It's the individualized and personalized approach of DAISY to deliver meaningful recognition to those nurses from patients and other nurses that makes it so important to them—and by extension the culture and morale of the hospital as a whole. In fact, when one hospital group that did not have the DAISY Award bought a hospital that did and then told the hospital to drop DAISY, they refused. But it also showed that organizations can change. Not only does the hospital that was acquired still have DAISY, but all but one in the system that bought it have added DAISY.

Not that we think DAISY is or will ever be for everybody. We know DAISY cannot honor everyone and thus have chosen not to be for everyone. For example, we heard certified nursing assistants and nursing techs were feeling left out of DAISY, and over the years we have gotten a lot of pressure either to include them as part of the awards or to create an award for them. These are very compassionate people no doubt and do provide hands-on care. But they are not nurses, and we decided not to change. We had to put a stake in the ground and say DAISY is for professional nurses. Our experience when Patrick was hospitalized was with nurses. Not CNAs or respiratory therapists or anyone else. It was Pat's nurses who inspired us to say thank you. If an organization wanted to recognize nursing assistants and nursing techs or other nonlicensed staff, then just like doctors they could be part of the Team Award. If an organization still wanted separate awards for different staff, they can create one. We are happy to share our model with anyone who asks—and we have! We helped a friend create the PHIL Award for outstanding respiratory therapists. And we salute all the awards hospitals have created to provide recognition to nonnursing employees who demonstrate compassion and dedication to patients.

That said, Mark created something to show gratitude for people who do something wonderful for us: the DAISY Founders' Coin. He loved the idea of the coin traditionally given in the military as a way for senior leaders to show their appreciation in a more tangible way than a spoken thank you. Our DAISY Founders' Coin says those words in writing: Our DAISY daisy on the front and just a simple THANK YOU on the back. Everyone we give them to is blown away by the gesture. The coins are also heavy and feel almost indestructible, because as Mark says, "A thank-you is indestructible."

❀ ❀ ❀

But let's get back to the nurses screwing up our turnkey operations. Next up was a hospital and their nurses that wanted to recognize their DAISY Coordinator. She was doing all the work for the program, like the arduous job of clearing the calendars of the hospital's leadership to be available when the nurse was being honored, blinding nominations (sometimes more than 100 a month), and getting the cinnamon rolls. She tended to the myriad details her committee came up with to make their award presentations so special. So we introduced the DAISY Champion. These champions are sometimes—but not always—administrative assistants or unit clerks who go above and beyond to make their DAISY programs the best they can be. The presentation allows *them* for once to be the ones who get to sit back and relish what it feels like to receive the recognition that they have made happen for so many nurses. Every champion gets a personal video message from Bonnie, and she has recorded hundreds of them. We get videos of the presentations to DAISY Champions, and we never tire of watching them.

Next up was the DAISY Faculty Award, which came out of a discussion with the board, which you might recall is made up of mostly nurses—nurses who clearly remain in cahoots with those screwing up our turnkey operations from outside the organization. In this case it was Beth Heyman, formerly of the Health Alliance of Greater Cincinnati and now dean of the Galen College of Nursing in Cincinnati, who said, "You know, somebody had to teach those nurses who took care of Patrick." Holy smokes! This was a real slap-in-the-forehead moment for us, considering our first award was delivered at a university hospital.

We'll be honest, though: As obvious as the idea was, this award did not take off the way the Nurse Leader and Team Awards would when they were introduced. We just couldn't get schools to accept it. The vast majority of deans we cold-called were not interested in recognition like this. They told us that for faculty, recognition was about presentations, publications, and tenure. As a result, we had fewer than 100 colleges of nursing after five years.

That all changed in May 2018 when we were traveling through Michigan during Nurse's Week. One of our stops was at the University of Michigan's nursing school, which had the faculty award program. We asked Dean Patty Hurn if we could meet their honorees, and she brought a bunch of them in to talk about what the DAISY Faculty Award meant to them. What one of them said impacted us deeply: "I was getting ready to retire and this award bought me five more years of teaching. When my students stood up and applauded for me when I was recognized with this DAISY Award, it meant the world to me." We knew right then we needed to invest a lot more energy into this program. We were acutely aware there was a real shortage of nursing faculty, because a lot of teachers were retiring. Faculty who remain in the hospitals and classrooms are on total overload. DAISY couldn't solve that, but it was clearly having some impact.

We asked Dean Hurn if she thought the American Association of Colleges of Nursing (AACN) would be the right organization to issue a national call to action for nursing faculty recognition. We had been collaborating with AACN since we started the Faculty Award, but growth had been really slow. Maybe if they heard why the DAISY Faculty Award had been so important to her, her faculty, and others we would ask to join us in this venture, we could get on AACN's agenda for their fall meeting. We would also approach Susan Groenwald to join us on our call with AACN. Susan was the president of Chamberlain University, a for-profit healthcare and nursing school that had campuses nationwide and an online program for all levels of nursing. Chamberlain's mission statement about creating compassionate nurses aligned with what DAISY was all about. They had become one of our industry partners and brought in DAISY soon after they learned about us. (Years later Susan invited us to speak at Chamberlain's graduation—a highlight of our speaking careers.)

In the end, we had six deans join us on a call to the AACN. Together we talked about how faculty recognition might help mitigate the very real issues facing nursing colleges—things like faculty burnout, retention, and retirements. AACN CEO Deb Trautman listened and agreed to issue the national call that October, after which we doubled the number of schools participating. We know we'll never get all 800 AACN members, but we're motivated to get as many as we can—and as many of the nurses granted associate degrees at schools that are members of the Organization of Associate Degree Nurses, which also supports DAISY faculty recognition. Because no matter what the future of nursing brings, the human touch will never be automated in our lifetimes. Robots may one day take over the world, but they are a long way from learning compassion—and for humans many schools still don't really teach compassion. Until they do, the DAISY Faculty

Award can help fill the void—for current and future teachers and nurses. Getting the new DAISY recognition programs going showed us why we had to remain students of nursing in order to continue to serve nurses everywhere. Which is why it should not be the least bit surprising that we also created an award for nursing students.

Shortly after we launched the DAISY Faculty Award, students at the University of Iowa sent us a PowerPoint presentation asking if we could add an award for them called the DAISY in Training Award. DAISY had been very successful at the University of Iowa Hospitals and Clinics for a long time, and the students had seen it there. We listened carefully to what these students had to say. They were concerned that with all the technology and clinical learning they were doing, they needed to be reminded why they wanted to be nurses in the first place. They knew nursing was not all clinical tasks and textbook learning. They were doing clinical rotations. They knew compassionate care had a profound impact on patients.

Another slap-your-forehead moment. We loved everything about the idea but the name. We changed it to the DAISY Award for Extraordinary Nursing Students. And while we were thinking about nurses at the start of their careers, why not add something at the end?

In 2018, Janet Rice, our DAISY Coordinator at UPMC Hamot, a hospital in Erie, Pennsylvania, asked if it would be okay if they honored a nurse who was retiring with a DAISY Award and a *Healer's Touch* sculpture as a gift. "She has worked here for 40 years," Janet said. "She has touched everything and every one of us. We have to do something for her. What would you think of a lifetime achievement award?"

"Duh," Mark replied.

"Why didn't we think of that?" Bonnie added.

Thus, the DAISY Lifetime Achievement Award was born, and it was a smash. We awarded more than 80 of them in 2019, its first full year.

❀ ❀ ❀

So you see, on our 20th anniversary, DAISY is no longer turnkey thanks to the nurses who have defined DAISY's evolution. But that's perhaps not the most important lesson that nurses taught us as they owned and expanded the reach of the foundation. We have always said nurses are nurses everywhere. The important lesson nurses have taught us is that a DAISY Nurse is a DAISY Nurse no matter what award they receive.

Yes, DAISY's awards are each different in some way, as are the *Healer's Touch* sculptures that go with them. The nurse leader *Healer's Touch* is a little larger with a small twist, compared to the original sculpture, to reflect the indirect care they give. The student award is a little smaller than the original. The Lifetime Achievement Award is a little larger than all of them and comes with a pin we had designed by a jeweler. The Team Honorees get a special plaque. Nurses didn't mind any of this. But to further distinguish the awards, we had initially divided all of them into two groups: The DAISY Award for Extraordinary Nurses and the DAISY Awards for everything else. But nurses didn't. No matter what award they received, they called it the DAISY Award. Because they saw it as the same award.

This was another epiphany to us. Maybe that means we're not as smart as we never thought we were. In all seriousness, it means that nurses made DAISY not just bigger and better but more complex than we could possibly have understood when we came up with the idea for DAISY at that liquid dinner. We don't just have these different awards in hospitals and nursing schools. We're in all kinds of clinics, healthcare organizations, staffing agencies, and businesses that employ nurses—places completely outside of our original vision, so every nurse anywhere has the opportunity to be recognized and celebrated by their nursing colleagues in front of their teams, physicians, coworkers, and many times the patients who nominate them. When their powerful stories of compassionate care, as told by those who nominate them, are read aloud for all to hear, they comprehend the impact they make every day. No matter the award, they tell us that receiving a DAISY was a meaningful milestone in their nursing careers. They enable us to understand the power of meaningful recognition that DAISY represents.

But nurses didn't just help us understand this anecdotally. They also gave DAISY evidence that meaningful recognition makes a difference.

DAISY HONOREE STORY

Amal Awni Mohammad, RN
King Hussein Cancer Center
Amman, Jordan

In 2020, my wife was diagnosed with thymoma. She has been receiving her treatment at King Hussein Cancer Center (KHCC) for almost three years. She was recently hospitalized in the Intensive Care Unit (ICU) due to a severe illness that had left her weak and bedridden. In fact, I want to express my sincere gratitude to all nurses at this unit, particularly a kind-hearted ICU nurse named Amal for the extraordinary care she provided to my wife throughout her stay in the unit.

Amal is actually an outstanding nurse. Her care and compassion toward her patients were unparalleled. Every day, I witnessed Amal's unwavering commitment and unrelenting dedication to providing exceptional care to my wife and other patients in the ICU. Her gentle touch, pleasant smile, and encouraging words gave my wife hope and support during this challenging time.

One day, as I sat by my wife's side, I noticed a photo frame on the bedside table. There were photos of my two children inside the frame. In fact, watching their smiling faces brought tears to my eyes as I yearned for my wife to recover and be reunited with our beloved children. So I asked Amal, "Where did you get this lovely frame? It really means a lot to us." Then Amal smiled warmly and started to share the touching story behind it. During her day off, Amal would often stroll through the gift shop; she spotted the photo frame and instantly thought of my wife, to brighten the ICU room. Knowing the importance of family and the healing power of love, she decided to buy it as a gift for her.

Amal revealed, "I saw the love in your wife's eyes whenever she spoke about her children, so I wanted her to be reminded of them, even when they couldn't be there physically, that is why I bought the frame for her. It's a simple gift, but I hoped it would bring her peace and comfort during her difficult times in the hospital."

"Amal's kindness and the photo frame she brought us will forever be etched in my heart," my wife stated. "She cared for me physically while also nourishing my spirit with her care and compassion. I will always remember her as the nurse who went above and beyond."

I thanked Amal for her consideration and care. I realized she wasn't simply an exceptional nurse, but also a compassionate soul who appreciated the value of reuniting patients with their loved ones.

Days and weeks passed, and Amal's loving care and sustained support uplifted my wife's spirit. Through her expertise and unshakable devotion, Amal not only provided nursing care but also created a healing environment packed with love and compassion. She ensured that my wife would never feel alone or discouraged throughout her hospital stay.

Actually, no words can express how I feel about such an exceptional nurse. Amal's compassionate care remained a guiding light for us, reminding us of the extraordinary influence that a single nurse can have on a patient's life. May God bless you.

I wrote these words in my and my family's names hoping to say, "Thank You, Amal." You deserve the honor and the distinction of being recognized as a DAISY Nurse.

"Every day we have multiple opportunities to recognize nursing excellence but in our busy schedules and fast-paced environments, we fail to do so. The DAISY Award helps us focus on this important aspect of our practice—celebrating nurses who provide compassionate, sensitive, and evidence-based care to patients and families."

Margie Sipe, DNP, RN, NEA-BC

Shining a New Light

The night Patrick involuntarily extubated his ventilator and blood went flying everywhere as the tube came out remains one of the most upsetting things we have ever seen or experienced. Tana, our nurse that night, took complete control of the situation—and us. And after she had everything reported and under control, she gave each of us a hug. That was the first time we learned that nurses give the best hugs.

Tana's hug is still with us today, as are the hugs of so many nurses we've met over the years. Countless other families and patients would say the same thing about their nurses' hugs. After all, hugs are the most human, physical manifestation of the relationship nurses have with patients and their families. They can mean as much as any act of compassion DAISY recognizes.

What hugs are *not* is scientific proof of the impact nurses make and the value of the meaningful recognition DAISY offered. And as DAISY grew, we began being asked for that, especially by nurse leaders and researchers. *Where is the evidence that shows meaningful recognition advances nursing practice? Where is the research that shows the DAISY Award will accomplish something significant for our staffs?* Evidence, evidence, evidence, evidence. Research, research, research, research. Even as we approached 1,000 hospitals, these words and questions about them followed us.

Not that we dismissed the need for evidence and research or their importance to nursing. We surely respected that in nursing, evidence-based practice means ensuring that patient care techniques are based on evidence grounded in scientific method. That's essential. But what makes nurses and nursing exceptional is a blend of clinical excellence and the art of compassion—the intuitive, intimate, real understanding of patients and families that comes from listening and paying attention to them. Nurses get this, especially DAISY Nurses, who have been honored by those patients and families. Yet even some DAISY Nurses were looking for research and evidence-based projects on meaningful recognition and how DAISY worked.

There was some evidence for the importance of meaningful recognition as DAISY grew. In 2005, the American Association of Critical-Care Nurses (AACN) cited meaningful recognition as one of six evidence-based standards for healthy and productive work environments along with skilled communication, true collaboration, effective decision making, appropriate staffing, and authentic leadership. "Nurses must be recognized and must recognize others for the value each brings to the work of the organization," the AACN stated at the time, and later reinforced with updated research in 2016. The AACN concluded that to be effective, recognition should be delivered through a formal process and program—exactly what DAISY does. But we were in our infancy when the AACN did its research. The standards affirmed the significance of what we did and aligned with the purpose of our work. But of the six AACN standards, meaningful recognition had the least amount of information and literature behind it.

With nurses owning and defining our direction more and more every day, we knew we needed to address this. But no metrics, let alone research studies or evidence-based projects, existed to even guide us on how to approach a study of the value of recognition for compassionate care. Our evidence was anecdotal, coming from the thousands of nurse leaders honoring their nurses and those nurses telling us about the feeling they got being honored with or just being nominated for a DAISY Award. How do you measure a feeling? How do you quantify a hug? It would be up to us to delve more deeply into the impact of our program for the evidence some nurses wanted and to better comprehend what DAISY was actually accomplishing for them and their organizations. Thanks to Dianne's work to capture the stories, we had thousands of nominations to explore. We just didn't know how to do it.

That's when the gods of nursing smiled on us once again: We met Cindy Lefton. Her work would provide the first evidence DAISY needed, and her words would inspire the title of this book.

❦ ❦ ❦

We first met Cindy at the 2008 AONE Annual Conference, our first time at a conference. We attended a session copresented by Laura Caramanica, then the chief nursing officer at Westchester Medical Center in New York, which was a DAISY partner. The presentation focused on nurses' satisfaction with support services like housekeeping, and was based on results from a survey that had been done at 42 hospitals including Westchester. When the session ended, we congratulated Laura on her presentation and told her how fascinated we were by the evidence she presented. We mentioned that we were looking to generate a more evidence-based understanding of DAISY's impact.

"We want to put some science behind DAISY," Bonnie said.

Standing next to Laura was a woman we had never met before listening intently. Laura pointed in her direction, "Talk to her."

The woman looked at us and said, as we recall, "I know we have never met but I know about your work. I'm an organizational psychologist and a trauma nurse. I think you're onto something here. I'd love to do that study for you."

Are you serious?

She said she was, and introduced herself as Cindy Lefton. She worked at Psychological Associates in St. Louis, a well-respected firm founded by her father that helps clients select, develop, and retain talent. "I was at AONE to go to a presentation we had been involved in for Westchester Medical Center and wanted to thank Laura who was one of the presenters," Cindy says today. "I was standing there while she was talking to Bonnie, and she looked at and then pointed to me and said, 'Talk to her.' But I don't know that I knew much about what the DAISY Foundation was because they were still pretty new. Bonnie and I continued talking as a result of that conversation, however, and we eventually gave them a proposal for something like $40,000. They were surprised, but Psychological Associates is a for-profit business. That's what the study was worth."

We told Cindy we couldn't afford that. While the idea of doing research was very exciting, as full-time volunteers with very lean finances that we had just stabilized by having organizations pay for DAISY, we didn't see how we could pay tens of thousands of dollars for a full-blown research study.

Then something miraculous happened. Cindy said, "Well, we'll just do it for free." We know that sounds incredible—almost unbelievable. Nope.

"The more I thought about the study, the more I realized it was really important. It needed to be done," Cindy recalls. "I'm a nurse, and I know nurses always get positive feedback from their patients. Even as healthcare pushes to get people out of the hospital quicker, those endearing relationships are created. They still matter. But until DAISY, the words were just spoken in some amazing situation and then the nurses went on to the next patient and the next one. It keeps going, and going, and going. Nurses don't really talk about our days to nonhealthcare people because it's too hard to explain, so all that feedback was getting lost. What researching DAISY allowed me to do was give a bigger voice to these thousands of patients and families who told these nurses how important they were—that they matter and that they make a difference. DAISY had all these nominations with all this powerful positive feedback, and people still weren't focusing on the power of positive feedback. It connected the dots between what nurses are doing right and why it matters."

In Cindy's opinion, nurses weren't spending enough time on the "right." Most of the time nurses are focused on the "wrong." What's wrong with this patient. What's wrong with this piece of equipment. What went wrong with this situation. Something goes wrong and nurses spend countless hours on root cause analyses. But what happens when something goes right? Nothing. No meeting to analyze it and consider the impact of the positive. DAISY captured that positive and made nurses stop and celebrate the things they do well not just from the clinical side but from the human side.

"The DAISY Award brings to light the right," Cindy said. Bringing to light the right. What a perfect way to say what DAISY does. Cindy would shine that light on what we do in a way we never could: applying organizational psychology principles and behavioral science to examine the positive feedback and meaningful recognition behind DAISY. We were awed not only by Cindy's connection to our work but by the scope of her study: 2,195 blinded DAISY Award nominations from 20 locations analyzed; 42 randomly selected DAISY Award Honorees and 21 chief nursing officers interviewed. Of course Cindy was only doing what she does so brilliantly and what was expected of her in the field. What she didn't expect was how moved she would be by her research—so moved that she decided to go back into nursing.

"I read every single nomination," Cindy remembers. "One night I was sitting in my office, reading. I'd never seen rich data like that. I have a little bit of a background in customer service. I'm sitting there looking at this thinking, 'If Walmart or FedEx had stuff like this, they'd go nuts.' I was so taken emotionally. I started to cry at one of the nominations because it was so beautiful. I thought, 'You know what? I belong back in the hospital.' I actually flipped my career at that point. I went from working full-time at Psychological Associates to working part-time there and being a nurse again part-time at a hospital."

Like most studies, Cindy's took years to complete, write up, and get published, but in late 2012, it finally came out: "Strengthening the Workforce Through Meaningful Recognition" appeared in the November-December issue of *Nursing Economic$*. The results were beyond our wildest dreams, the effect impossible to overstate. Cindy's study changed the way DAISY was perceived by the broader nursing community. It put the strength of research behind what we had said from the beginning: Giving patients, families, and coworkers a way to genuinely express gratitude for the extraordinary compassionate care they received meant more to nurses and organizations than just the award itself.

❀ ❀ ❀

The first point in Cindy's executive summary said it all: "Meaningfully recognizing the extraordinary contributions of nurses is a key element in creating and sustaining healthy work environments." Her study broke that down into four key findings:

1. The meaningful recognition process can elevate the value of nursing by providing patients, family members, and colleagues with a vehicle to recognize the extraordinary work of nurses.

2. Through a formalized meaningful recognition process, patients, family members, and colleagues can provide in their own words real-time feedback describing what mattered to them during their hospitalization and identify how behaviors of an extraordinary nurse made a difference.

3. Providing patients, families, and peers with a process to recognize nurses in a meaningful manner augments patient satisfaction data by illuminating the "detail" associated with these scores.

4. Formally recognizing extraordinary nursing through celebration can assist in shaping and driving an organization's culture and strengthening one's workforce.

"Whether it's shock and awe, demonstrating pride in one's work, nourishing a team, reaffirming the ministry of nursing, realizing the value of one's contributions, or reigniting a person's career," Cindy wrote, "this research provides the evidence that meaningful recognition can indeed strengthen a workforce."

We will never forget reading those words. For the first time we had an understanding of not just what it meant for us to say thank you to nurses but what it meant to the nurses to be thanked. Those four points transformed the way DAISY was perceived by nurse-researchers and anyone in nursing and beyond who wanted a side of science with all they were seeing in and feeling from the DAISY Awards. They reached chief nursing officers who needed more proof that DAISY would accomplish something significant for their staffs. As an experienced qualitative researcher, Cindy's expert insight into our nomination stories showed how they reflected what patients truly value and painted a vivid picture of what "extraordinary" care looks like. Themes of compassion, contagious positive attitude, calming presence, and connection to the family were among the top ten themes she identified. These nomination themes focused on *how* care was provided and what it meant.

A mom of a frightened child recalls how her sick little girl was distracted by her nurse who sang songs from *Frozen* to her while he handled her difficult IV insertion. This calmed her daughter and gave the mom a sense of trust that the nurse really cared about her child. A dressing change for a seriously burned man describes how his nurse knew how to minimize his extreme pain. The nurse listened to the patient, taking special care to do it in the exact way the patient could handle. An inspirational quote delivered by a nurse to a suicidal, depressed, and deeply anxious veteran patient showed the respect this person deserved and inspired him to work to get better. Because the nurse wanted to make a difference in the lives of those who have served our country.

Shining the Light on All the Right

These stories and thousands of others show how DAISY Honorees stand as role models, providing exemplars of nursing practice that can be used to set expectations for performance—for clinical competence and also for the human connection that is at the core of nursing practice. The science and the art of nursing, the delicate balance that makes a great difference to a patient's care experience. Care that other nurses are inspired to emulate.

Cindy's research also showed that the DAISY Awards enriched patient satisfaction scores because they provided organizations a treasure trove of qualitative data. When those organizations took the time to celebrate the "right" going on and implemented an ongoing, structured program of meaningful recognition like DAISY, it transcended the limitations and deepened their understanding of their quantitative patient satisfaction survey scores. After all, how do you put a "1 to 5" score on a patient writing "My nurse gave me the will to live"?

Cindy's final point about strengthening the workforce and its connection to DAISY was perhaps the most rewarding point to us as it showed how our recognition program contributes to the emotional rewards for nurses around the country. Nurses and especially nurse leaders constantly told us their DAISY Award celebrations—not just their own DAISY Awards but those for every nurse celebrated at the organization—were the best part of their days. Sharing nurses' stories throughout the year in a formal setting with an integrity-rich structure reminded nurses why they became nurses, toiled in nursing school, worked shifts they didn't probably didn't choose to work early in their careers, and dealt with the myriad pressures that healthcare is throwing at them day in and day out. Knowing that patients, family members, or colleagues took the time to write their stories of compassionate care made unbearable days a little more bearable for them. DAISY's meaningful recognition could not affect the concerning national trend of nursing shortages, but now we at least knew how it could help retain nurses already in the workforce. Cindy knew on a personal and scientific level how desperately that was and is needed.

"People are pretty tired," Cindy says, thinking about her work today. "The turnover in new nurses is just horrific. When I see them clocking out at the end of a 12-hour shift with that look in their eye, that they're so tired and they don't feel like they've made a difference . . . it saddens me that they don't realize the difference that they have made. Workplace violence is very prevalent, particularly in emergency departments. There's a lot of challenges with people who have behavioral health issues because there's not enough facilities across the country. No nurse should ever walk out at the end of their shift without recognizing something good that they did—the difference that they made in somebody's life. DAISY is nursing's best cheerleader."

Actually patients and families are nursing's best cheerleaders. We humbly facilitate a program that enables their stories to be shared and recognizes all the good that is happening every day. But before Cindy's study, we had no way to shine a scientific light on how DAISY has changed cultures to emphasize acts of compassionate care. Now we had a new tool in our toolbox: a research study to show how meaningful recognition advances nursing practice and how nurses are inspired to advance their practice through DAISY. And Cindy's study wouldn't be the last.

※ ※ ※

After Cindy Lefton's study was published and presented at the Magnet conference, AONE's annual meeting, the AACN's National Teaching Institute, and elsewhere, a robust body of evidence demonstrating DAISY's impact was built—studies on the impact of meaningful recognition on a healthy work environment, nurse engagement, compassion fatigue and compassion satisfaction, how recognition affects the patient and family experience, and more.

Cindy and Lesly Kelly completed a mixed-method study to explore DAISY's impact on compassion fatigue. Cindy's qualitative portion interviewed 90-plus ICU nurses on what recharges their emotional energy. Four themes emerged: Nurses are recharged emotionally when they are thanked; see their patients improve clinically; know their team members have their back; and become aware that they have made a difference they didn't know they had made. The DAISY Award covered three of these four themes. The quantitative portion of this research, led by Lesly, revealed, among other things, that nurses who had received nominations for DAISY Awards had lower compassion fatigue and higher compassion satisfaction.

Chamberlain University did a study on the DAISY Faculty Award and their president, Susan Groenwald, cited it in her book *Designing & Creating a Culture of Care for Students and Faculty*. There is research that connects the kind of meaningful recognition DAISY offers as it relates to an organization's return on investment: A study by Laura McClellan and Timothy Vogus out of Virginia Commonwealth University found that "when a hospital explicitly rewards compassionate acts by its staff and supports its staff during tough times, it is associated with patients more highly rating the care experience and being more likely to recommend the hospital." And there are several studies in the works as we head into our 21st year, including the national rollout of a pilot study that Cindy Lefton did with Susan Grant, Cindy Sweeney (DAISY's vice president for nursing), and Melissa Foreman-Lovell. The pilot addressed a question we had been asking for several years: What does it mean to patients and families to say thank you to their nurses by writing a DAISY nomination? The findings of the pilot study show that patients and families feel connected to the organization through the nomination and recognition of their nurse, which may contribute to loyalty for the organization and increased likelihood to recommend it as a healthcare organization of choice.

There are many more studies we could cite here, not that we or the organizations that have implemented DAISY *need* more evidence. The primary goal of additional evidence is understanding: to shine the scientific and artistic light on all the right that nurses do and help those who don't see that right in themselves—or in each other. The additional goal is also for DAISY and all who work for and connect to us after twenty years to understand and articulate our impact. To that end, we developed what we call the DAISY Model of Impact.

The model was inspired by Cindy Sweeney, whom we hired in 2014. We had known Cindy since 2009 from ANCC, where she had been a director and run the Magnet conference. Her nursing and research background allowed her to use all we knew about DAISY to express as simply as possible how, as a form of meaningful recognition, DAISY can impact the organization. Cindy sketched on the back of an envelope what became the three "sides" of DAISY's triangle of impact: a Healthy Work Environment, Nurse Engagement, and the Patient/Family Experience. Each of these sides was informed by all the evidence we had and would receive in the years to come.

But while all three sides of the triangle are essential to the impact of DAISY's meaningful recognition on the nurses and the organizations we support, for all of us it always comes back to the stories—stories of nurses who are proficient in the relational aspects of nursing. Who understand how their care profoundly affects their patients and families and moves the patient/family experience into the realm of the extraordinary. Cindy Sweeney, Bonnie, and Mary Koloroutis said exactly that as the authors of DAISY's first white paper in 2015, "Inspiring Nurses to See the Extraordinary in the Ordinary." Yes, nurses will say what they often say when presented with a DAISY Award, "I was just doing my job—I was just doing what I do every day." They don't see the extraordinary in their ordinary. But you can't even spell extraordinary without ordinary.

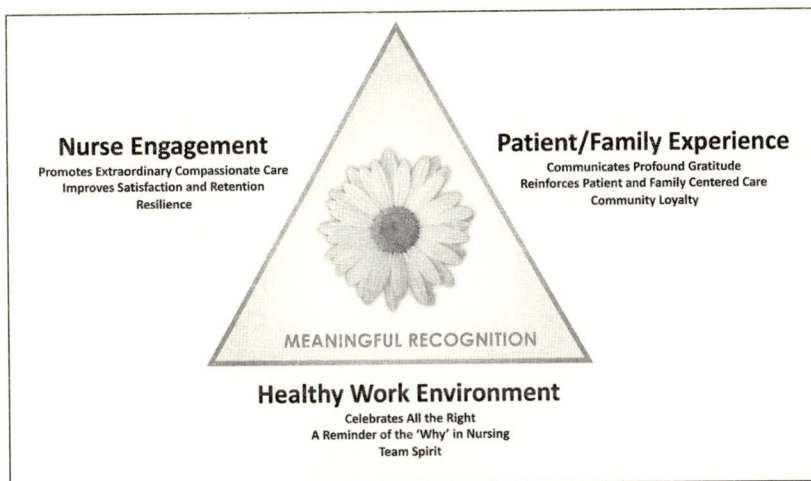

Nurse Engagement
Promotes Extraordinary Compassionate Care
Improves Satisfaction and Retention
Resilience

Patient/Family Experience
Communicates Profound Gratitude
Reinforces Patient and Family Centered Care
Community Loyalty

MEANINGFUL RECOGNITION

Healthy Work Environment
Celebrates All the Right
A Reminder of the 'Why' in Nursing
Team Spirit

The DAISY Impact Model

Cindy Lefton said one of her favorite stories she tells in her speeches is about an older terminally ill patient who only wanted a fruit plate. The way this woman described the importance of this fruit plate when she was nearing the end of her life showed how such a small thing can be so important. One nurse made sure she had it when she wanted it and was honored with a DAISY Award for her compassion. She was shocked. It was just a fruit plate. It was no big deal to arrange for it. Yet the nomination noted that several other nurses *didn't* do it before she did. The DAISY Nurse understood its importance, and hopefully in seeing her being presented her award, the other nurses who missed how little things make a difference will understand it, too.

Simply put: Many, many nurses and healthcare professionals don't need a white paper, research study, or evidence-based project to understand the significance of that nurse who delivered the fruit plate and hundreds of thousands, if not millions, of other nurses who perform those compassionate acts every day. We never appreciated this more than when we spoke at the Royal College of Surgeons School of Nursing and Midwifery in Dublin, Ireland. Most of the speakers who preceded us were scientific nurses doing wonderful talks on their very important research. They all received robust rounds of applause. When we spoke about DAISY, we did not focus on our research. We told our story and the stories of the nurses who received DAISY Awards. To our shock we received a standing ovation. Thomas Kearns, executive director of the Faculty of Nursing and Midwifery of the Royal College, explained why: "Some things you don't need the scientific evidence for. Some things are just so obviously right to do."

From the very beginning of DAISY, our goal was to express our heartfelt personal appreciation for the difference nurses made in our lives and the lives of their patients and their patients' families. Nurses make a big difference in the lives of others, so we did our best to make a difference in theirs. Nothing makes us prouder than to have stayed true to that mission.

DAISY HONOREE STORY

Anna Staniecki, BSN, RN
Melanie Suga, RN
LewisGale Medical Center
Salem, Virginia

My mother was hospitalized, and I found myself back in the surgical intensive care unit of LewisGale Hospital after almost ten years. Being in the unit again brought forth a flood of memories from years ago. After a month in the surgical intensive care unit, my husband, Joe, died there early on a Tuesday morning. While many of these memories are quite painful, there are also memories that I will forever cherish. These are memories of the people who worked so hard to care for my husband while very ill.

On Tuesday of this past week, my dear friend Anna Staniecki was with me at my mother's bedside and we began remembering ten years ago. Anna still works for LewisGale and I asked if any of Joe's nurses were also still working here.

Incredibly Melanie Suga was on duty that afternoon. She was a nurse that took care of Joe during the late night–early morning hours, and I will never forget her kindness. As I told the stories of what Anna and Melanie did for my husband Joe, we all started to cry. This conversation is what brings me here today to recognize the very special nurses for what they did for my husband and to say Thank You for the precious memories you have given me that help to ease the pain of what was a difficult time in my life.

During the latter part of Joe's time here, he was very restless and couldn't understand what was wrong and why we couldn't go home. He begged quite often for a few simple things. He asked me if I could find his pants. He said if I parked the car close and we found his pants, he thought we could make it out of here! He begged for coffee. He wanted to sleep with me again and he begged to see his very special little buddy, our dog, Cotton. Thanks to the nurses who heard his cries, Joe got almost all of his wishes.

Around 2:00 a.m., his last Saturday morning, the phone rang at home. It was Joe. I heard this very small, breathy voice ask "What are you doing?" I said, "Just thinking about you." Then Joe asked "Can you come over?" I told him to let me speak to Melanie. I asked Melanie if I could come over and get in bed with him. She said, "Of course." And she suggested that I bring a pillow sprayed with my perfume.

When I arrived at his bedside, Melanie had already given Joe a bath and moved all of his tubes and fluid collection bottles out of the way. And she had pulled Joe to one side of the bed so there was room for me. As I crawled in with him, Melanie left and pulled the curtain shut. Joe hadn't slept for days. But with me beside him, he finally fell into a deep sleep. And a day later, he was still holding that pillow spayed with my perfume.

Melanie, this may have been inconsequential to you, but it was very important to me and it was to Joe. It gave him peace and it fulfilled one of his final wishes. I am forever grateful to you for that and I will always remember you for your kindness.

Since it was against the hospital rules for Joe to see Cotton, those who assisted with breaking those rules will remain nameless, but this is a story you should hear. Growing up, Joe was never allowed to have a dog. Joe grew up in a hotel because his parents owned the hotel. He had never had a dog. So it was quite the surprise one Christmas when Joe went to the SPCA and selected Cotton for just me. The bond between them grew very strong. And while Joe was hospitalized, he missed Cotton terribly. So after hearing Joe's cries to see his little buddy again, the nameless group of cohorts went to work and a plan was hatched. Then on the Sunday before Joe's death, at the appointed time, Joe was taken to the outpatient entrance, and I met them with Cotton. My mother suggested I take some treats for Joe to feed him. Cotton weighed about 40 pounds and was typically full of life. But at that time, Cotton sat quietly beside Joe, smelling him and eating treats from his hand. It was as if he knew.

It was a beautiful day, the sun was shining, and the cohorts noticed Joe straining to see out. Someone asked him if he wanted to go outside. He said "Yes." So they rolled him out into the fresh air and he felt the warmth of the sunshine one last time.

I didn't know my dear friend Anna until I met her here ten years ago. I believe that God does know what is best for us. He knew that while everyone else was taking care of Joe, I needed someone to support me and help me to understand what was happening. Anna was a case manager back then. Sometime shortly after Joe's second surgery, someone was explaining the newest complications of his situation to me. I felt like I was going to faint. Then I felt these arms behind me and a voice asking if I needed a room and a chaplain. I said yes and was escorted to a private area. That person behind me was Anna. Throughout that month, whenever I needed support, or help, or just a warm, friendly smile that reassured me everything would be okay, I would look up and there was Anna. And she's been my dear friend ever since. It's impossible to describe all the goodness Anna has brought to my life. Anna is the angel that God sent to me when he knew I needed a true lifelong friend. Anna, your friendship has been a blessing in my life. Thank you for just being you and for the joy and peace you gave to Joe.

These women serve as examples of how nurses have a lasting impact on the lives of others. They are examples for the rest of us to follow. My life and Joe's final days were forever changed because of the caring, compassionate acts of Melanie Suga and Anna Staniecki, and I am so pleased to honor them with the DAISY Award.

"There is such powerful transformation that occurs for each nurse who learns that he/she was nominated and then even more so for the monthly recipient. The DAISY Award provides us with an opportunity to pause each month on a unit with the winner and peers and share how 'simple' nursing actions, caring, listening, and acknowledging are so critical to our patients and families."

Katherine Pakieser-Reed, PhD, RN

All We Wanted to Do Was Say Thank You

After a 2019 speaking engagement and dinner in Maine, we had to drive from Central Maine Medical Center in Lewiston to a bed-and-breakfast owned by a nurse in Bridgeton. The drive was only 35 miles inland, but we had spent well over an hour trying to find our way through the middle-of-Maine night. The same darkness that enveloped us also enveloped the navigation apps on our devices.

We were with our Northeast Regional Program Director, Alex Schoen, and each of us was using a different GPS. At each stop sign, Apple, Garmin, and Google told us to go in a different direction until we came to a fork in the road. Yogi Berra famously said when you come to a fork in the road, take it. Not even Yogi could help us now. All our devices said take the dirt road between the branches of the fork. It was 9:30 P.M. We could see nothing around us. We decided to trust what we saw and took the road less travelled—and unmarked—and ended up right where we belonged.

So has DAISY. We chose to take an unpaved and unmarked road to recognizing the nurses who had been so kind and delivered such compassionate care to us, our family, and Our Patrick in the weeks before he died.

Over the years, people have told us that choosing to emphasize this compassion in our recognition for nurses was an "innovation," but we didn't see it as all that inventive. All we wanted to do was say thank you. But unlike that night in Maine, we had no idea where we were going when we started—and no GPS could help us. Nothing like the DAISY Awards existed in the nursing world. We never imagined that 20 years later more than 4,000 organizations and colleges of nursing in the United States and 25 other countries would share our mission. At one point we didn't think we would make 50 hospitals in five years! We never intended to create DAISY Awards in six different categories. We never expected to have research studies published about the impact of our meaningful recognition—and to publish our own. Sure, we envisioned grants to support research—but to find a cure for ITP, not the myriad research of 100-plus nurse-led studies. That we would have a staff of 22 and 15 board members over the years supporting us and nurses still amazes us every day.

And we certainly never dreamed that we would receive more than 1.6 million DAISY Award nominations and honor 136,000 individuals and teams and counting by the end of our 20th year. Clearly, we were not the only family compelled to say thank you to nurses.

❀ ❀ ❀

The vastness of DAISY today is hard for us to comprehend and even accept sometimes. We still don't quite know what to make of people saying DAISY has transformed the culture of their organizations. Or when someone calls us rock stars. Every year we find ourselves standing in front of audiences of esteemed, highly educated nurses of all walks who are dedicated to improving the care of patients and wonder what the heck are we doing there. How did we become honorary members of Sigma Theta Tau International Honor Society of Nursing, the second-largest nursing organization in the world? How do we deserve to be honorary fellows of the American Academy of Nursing? Or honorary members of the American Organization for Nursing Leadership, the Oncology Nursing Society, and the Association of Pediatric/Hematology Oncology Nurses? Recipients of the Pioneering Spirit Award of the American Association of Critical-Care Nurses, American Nurses Credentialing Center's (ANCC's) President's Award, and so many more we have accepted with a mix of honor and incredulity? How did we end up being saluted by ANCC in front of 10,000-plus nurses with a song performed by Lexi Walker and the Opera Orlando Chorus at the 2019 Magnet conference in celebration of our 20th anniversary?

Recognizing the recognition DAISY provides: Our embrace in front of nurses at the tribute to DAISY at ANCC's Magnet Conference in honor of our 20th anniversary, October 2019. Photo by Kenneth Krehbiel, Imageworks Photography.

Nurses giving us standing ovations—thanking *us*? DAISY may exist because of us, but DAISY prospered in our first 20 years because of nurses!

In those moments of disbelief, we stand backstage, hold each other's hands, push down any feeling that someone has made a terrible mistake, and walk out together as our names are announced. Well, all but the one at the American Academy of Nursing. Mark still kept thinking as we took the stage that these were the smartest smarty-pants of the nursing world and maybe they weren't as smart as we thought they were because they were honoring *us*—and as a couple, which had never happened before.

That day at the Academy we felt a tremendous physical closeness as we took in DAISY's acceptance and embrace by this profession for what we brought them. But as we said that day and every day before and since, DAISY is a two-way street, and nurses brought us more than we feel we brought them. Nurses not only took ownership of DAISY but defined and evolved it, doing more things than we could possibly recount in these pages. They developed DAISY display walls, DAISY carts for presentations, DAISY-reserved parking places, specially designed DAISY nomination boxes (one cleverly crafted to look like a Cinnabon), DAISY elevator door coverings, and DAISY cakes and cookies. Nurses made DAISY nomination signs for patients' rooms, to post throughout the hospital, to go home in discharge packets, and to post on their organizations' websites. They have DAISY-fied every article of clothing we could imagine from T-shirts to sweatshirts to aprons to jackets. We've seen DAISY badge pulls, lanyards, water bottles, coffee cups, balloons, and . . . ice sculptures! Then the nurses spread awareness of all this DAISY-fication by putting it and more on Facebook, Instagram, Twitter, YouTube, and every other form of social media we don't know anything about.

Yes, one time the nurses' creativity almost cost us a lot of money when their hospital placed a picture of a field of daisies on its nomination form. We thought it was gorgeous so we copied the photo and sent it out to all the hospitals at the time to use. Turns out it wasn't their photo. They'd copied it from a stock photo company that contacted

Cinnamon roll DAISY nomination box, Morton Plant Mease
Health Care, Clearwater, FL

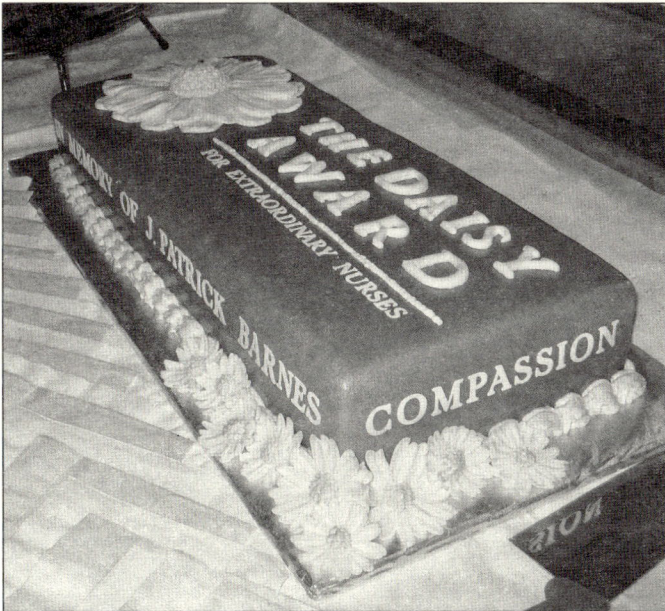

DAISY cake baked by the daughter of a nurse for Thomas Jefferson
University Methodist Hospital, Philadelphia

DAISY elevators, Lower Keys Medical Center, Key West, FL

us and asked for $30,000 for permission to use it in all the hospitals. Thankfully they settled for $300. (Someone there probably had a story of an extraordinary nurse.)

Most of the time, however, the creativity just makes us smile and costs nothing, like the DAISY Award ceremony at Grady Memorial in downtown Atlanta. When we visited years ago, Rhonda Scott, then the chief nursing officer, gathered her senior leaders for every DAISY presentation and they carried pompoms and a boom box through the hospital to surprise the DAISY Nurse by playing Tina Turner's "Simply the Best." Nurses have also welcomed us in unforgettable ways, like at Bronson Methodist Hospital in Kalamazoo, Michigan. The nurses gathered in a room filled with daisy plants, and after the award presentation, they picked up the flowers and planted them in a DAISY garden.

Like the daisies in that garden today, DAISY got here because of nurses. We thrive because of the nurse leaders who tell us what DAISY means to them; how the days DAISY is on their calendars are their favorite days of the month; and how their DAISY Honorees' stories make them indescribably proud of their staffs as they marvel at their compassion and excellence. We succeed because of the DAISY Coordinators and DAISY Committees who are dedicated to bringing our program to life month after month when they have oh-so-much-else to do. The nurses and others who fill those roles are passionate about DAISY and bring their creativity and resourcefulness to ensure its success in their organizations. They care so much for the nurses on their staffs and know they deserve to have every DAISY Award presentation be an unforgettable experience.

And of course we got here because of the extraordinary care provided by and recognized in our DAISY Award Honorees and Nominees. When we ask them why they committed their lives to nursing, what they talk about is taking care of patients. Of being in that sacred, trusted space when people are at their most vulnerable. We can see that their outstanding clinical judgment and expertise, honed over years of education, training, and experience, is inextricably linked to the compassionate care we so profoundly admire and celebrate. Nurses even tell us they hold—and must remember to hold—themselves differently when they become DAISY Nurses. One nurse told us that soon after she received her award she was having a bad day and feeling grumpy. One of the other nurses said, "You can't act like that anymore. You're a DAISY Nurse." These words really resonated with her, and she realized she had to hold herself to a higher standard—that a DAISY Award came with extra responsibility and accountability.

❀ ❀ ❀

DAISY has come with new responsibility and accountability for us, too. We see ourselves as DAISY's facilitators, but also its gatekeepers. Mark never fails to ask questions about any innovation, award, partnership, sponsorship, and relationship no matter how perfect it seems to align with what we do. *Do we want to do this? Is this in line with our message? Is this DAISY?* We have been very clear about our strategy for anyone who wants to work with us. First and foremost they have to love nurses. Any conversation that mentions the importance of return on investment, not an appreciation of all nurses do, gets politely shut down. The value of DAISY is implicit in the meaningful recognition we offer, and we are looking for relationships based on an understanding of that. We have discontinued and rejected sponsors that didn't get this—or just didn't feel right. We believe staying true to these principles and our mission is why DAISY has a remarkable 96 percent retention rate. Even organizations that get sold or hospitals that merge with a larger group that doesn't have DAISY have stayed with us.

Our private life is also accountable to DAISY. We may aggressively discuss where we are going or how someone or something is doing—we have our challenges all the time just like any family and family business. But it is always based in gratitude and love for DAISY and each other—and respect. We made a deal at the beginning of this journey that whenever one of us had an idea, the other one had to respect it and work to implement it. That said, Bonnie will tell you she couldn't keep up with Mark's ideas. Bonnie's the thinker—the writer and public speaker. She may cry at every new DAISY creation she sees, but she leads with her head. Mark may ask all those questions and be the business strategist for DAISY, but he leads with his heart. It's a balance that has allowed us to grow DAISY together without "killing" each other. We could not love it or each other more. DAISY is our passion and we share it with the world, *together*. In fact, we don't do anything DAISY without doing it together; most people never see us apart. One time Bonnie had to go to a conference alone because a dog had bit Mark and he couldn't travel. This was quite disorienting for the attendees, and Bonnie spent all four days answering one question: "Where's Mark?"

People those days may have wondered where Mark was, but like that night driving in Maine, we can say with absolute certainty that we, like DAISY, have ended up right where we belong: at home with the nurses.

And still to this day, those nurses will tell us everything we experienced with Patrick was just them doing their jobs. That it was nothing special. We want to say one last time that when you are a patient or a family member, in a heightened state of emotion and feeling helpless and quite scared and you watch a great nurse in action, the work they do is special. It's sacred. It's meaningful. It makes a difference and has an impact. It deserves recognition. It deserves respect.

Our greatest hope is that DAISY somewhere, somehow makes one more person realize the power of meaningful recognition—to a nurse for sure, but also to a colleague, stranger, friend, loved one, or someone who simply did something right by you. If we can put one more genuine, heartfelt thank-you in this world, then we have shone a little more light on the right people do. The importance of genuine, authentic recognition for even the little things people do, without any expectation of return, to make your life or the life of someone you love better, is something that cannot be discounted in this world. It seems so easy to do but we are all so pressed for time and thinking about what is going wrong that we forget the power of a simple thank-you.

Twenty years after our liquid dinner, we couldn't imagine a life without DAISY, even though it meant we had to accept that we had lost Our Patrick. But we have been comforted by the feeling that he is with us in spirit and proud of all DAISY has become. He would be thrilled that people still know his name and his story. And we know what he would say to us if he could. They're the same words he would say to all his nurses: *Thank you.*

DAISY HONOREE STORY

Lauren Sanchez, BSN, RN
Kaiser Permanente Anaheim Medical Center
Anaheim, California

One of our patients with COVID-19 [had] been on the ventilator in the DOU [Definitive Observation Unit] for several days. Her husband, recovering from COVID at home, would call the unit every day and request for the nurse to assist in doing a FaceTime with his wife. We encouraged him to talk to her and explained that even though she is sedated, she could still hear him. So every day he called, and we used the phone so he could see her. He would talk to her and give her some encouraging words.

One day he mentioned to Lauren Sanchez, RN, the patient's nurse, that he drives from home to the hospital and sits in his car in the parking lot for hours just to feel close to his wife. Lauren advised him that his wife's room overlooks an area above the cafeteria. She suggested to him that she would cut out a pink heart and post it in her window to identify her room. The pink heart would let him know what room she was in and so he could sit closer to the unit downstairs and look at the heart in the window and feel even closer to her. The patient's husband sat outside in the atrium for three hours that day and stared at the pink heart posted in the window of her room. He was so thankful for the gesture. He said that even though he couldn't hold or see her, he felt close to her looking at the pink heart two floors up.

This was an easy decision for Lauren, an expression of the love she was now unable to share physically with her family and loved ones at home, [because of] the situation created by the COVID pandemic: "It is such a heartbreaking choice to be away from my daughter and husband. But that's the choice I must make to provide the best care to our critically ill patients. I miss my family dearly and I try to translate some of my love for my family into each and every one of my patients."

Here is how I reported the husband's account of the kind gesture in an email to our leaders: "Mr. M, whose wife is your patient, also raved about the nurses and doctors. In particular, he asked me to make sure that Nurse Lauren Sanchez received recognition. Mr. M. said that Nurse Sanchez went 'above and beyond' to make this horrible situation a little bit better. He started to sob as he described Nurse Sanchez hanging a heart on his wife's window so that he could see it. He also said that Nurse Sanchez patiently helped him FaceTime with his wife. Although the patient can't talk, Nurse Sanchez said things like 'Squeeze my hand if you heard your husband say I love you.' Nurse Sanchez reported to Mr. M that the patient squeezed his hand. He just kept saying that everyone was super nice. He was 'more than satisfied.' He felt that Nurse Sanchez was exceptional, and he couldn't say enough good about her."

Nursing Our Future
2020–2024

> *When a project connects to your purpose, it makes the work that much more fulfilling. At the core, the ripple effect of the DAISY Award, and the impact it has on so many different levels, is almost immeasurable.*
>
> Christopher Wojnar, BSN, RN

Fire

Flashback to Friday, October 6, 2017. We had been at a conference in San Antonio and were scheduled to be in Houston on Tuesday. We debated whether we should just spend the weekend in Texas and visit friends but decided to go home for the weekend.

The fires started on Sunday night.

Our first clue something was wrong was around midnight when one of our German shepherds, Max, started barking his head off. Max barks at things outside all the time, but not at night. We looked out the window and saw the orange glow of fire at the end of our vineyard behind the house. We thought it was a grass fire. Shaking off our sleep, we went outside to get hoses to put it out. The hoses didn't even have nozzles on them. We planned to use our thumbs to make a spray. Then we noticed trees were burning too, and the neighbor's lawn in flames. This was no grass fire. And it was coming towards us.

☀ ☀ ☀

Bonnie tried calling 911 from her cell. Busy signal. They answered on the second try. The fire department arrived in minutes because they were posting a blockade at the end of our road. We were loading the dogs in the car as a fireman tromped across the yard in full equipment.

"Get out of here right now. Get in your cars, close the garage doors, and leave. We will try to save your house."

We grabbed the dogs and left. Our friends Joan and Jim Griffin took us in at their house in Petaluma. The next morning we all began to grasp the enormity of what would be known as the Northern California Wildfires of 2017: 250 of them that would eventually consume 250,000 acres that October in just four counties. The fires raged all Monday in our area of Sonoma Valley but by Tuesday they had shifted away, and we decided to try to get to our house to see what had become of it. We drove to the blockade with Erin Ascher, DAISY's executive assistant. The air was hideous, rancid and acrid, not the clean wood smoke of a campfire. No one could tell us if our house had survived.

We talked our way past the police, and as we walked up the hill toward our house, the scene that unfolded was more hideous than the air. It looked like our entire neighborhood had burned down. We got to the bottom of our driveway and started up, dreading what we might see. As we came around the bend, we saw our garage, which served as DAISY's warehouse and shipping department, was gone. Our hearts sank as we kept walking to the house. But it was safe—badly scorched in places, but safe. We looked back to where the garage had been. That's when we saw them. Surrounded by smoldering trees from the woods that used to be there and amidst the ashes and rubble of the garage, eight of the large *Healer's Touch* sculptures. More than 400 hospitals and organizations had bought these to display in their lobbies and healing gardens as a tribute to the care their nurses provide. Prior to the fire, they were packed in their wooden crates, ready to be shipped. The crates had burned, but the stone carvings were standing tall and strong. *Look at that!*

"This is a sign," Erin said.

⁕ ⁕ ⁕

What it was a sign of we had no time to process. The wind was picking up. We knew the fires could come back. We grabbed the stuff we needed from inside the house, used water from the jugs we stored on the porch to put out hot spots that were all over the place, and left once again.

The fires did come back, threatening the home Mark had lived in since 1970. But we thought about DAISY as much as we thought about anything else in there—our home and DAISY's were one and the same. More than 1,000 *Healer's Touch* sculptures and everything else that goes with the DAISY Awards that had been stored in the garage were already gone. They were replaceable, but inside the house were our offices, and Mark's was the DAISY Museum. Every shelf, cabinet, and bit of wall space and floor space was filled with the one-of-a-kind, irreplaceable artifacts we had received and collected since DAISY's beginning. Everything the nurses, hospitals, colleges, and other organizations around the world had given us. Every award, letter, scrapbook, gift, and tchotchke. All we could do was pray the fires wouldn't cost us any more than they already had.

They didn't.

Our house had caught fire, but the firefighters had put it out before it could do tragic damage. The hillsides all around our home and most of our neighbors' houses were incinerated. We were among the lucky ones. Nevertheless, we couldn't move back for six weeks until the fires were extinguished for good, power was restored, and a 2,500-gallon temporary water tank was delivered and hooked up. We could visit, though, and every time we did, we saw those large *Healer's*

After the fire, *Healer's Touch* sculptures standing tall amid the rubble, October 2017

Touch sculptures on the burn pile. We thought about Erin calling them a sign. But of what? A phoenix, of course—DAISY rising from the ashes! The phoenix analogy seemed perfect—and, we realized, wrong. DAISY was not a phoenix, because DAISY had not died upon this pyre. If everything we owned had burned to the ground that October, our loss would be personally devastating, but DAISY would stand tall and strong like those *Healer's Touch* sculptures. DAISY was alive and well in offices and organizations around the world. The sculptures were not a sign of DAISY's rebirth. They were a sign of DAISY's resilience. We didn't need to keep DAISY going. DAISY *was* going . . . in Georgia, Washington, Michigan, Ohio, Maryland, Oklahoma, and other parts of California—states where our remarkable staff live—and in the hands of nurses at thousands of hospitals and organizations worldwide. They, like the intertwined figures in the sculptures, were holding DAISY up.

❀ ❀ ❀

We may have lovingly called our offices in our Sonoma home the DAISY Worldwide Headquarters, but DAISY had been more than Mark and

Bonnie Barnes for years. Long before the fires burned, we told our board that we trusted them to keep DAISY going long after we are gone. They assured us DAISY would live on in their hands and in their hearts. But so have our family, staff, the organizations that support us, and most importantly the nurses all over the world who would never let DAISY go. We heard those assurances over and over again from the nurses who reached out in the days and weeks following the fires to make sure we were okay. Their words lifted us up as we rebuilt and restocked. The messages made us feel that we were not just okay—we were strong and resilient. And so was DAISY. In response to all those wonderful messages, and to reach as many nurses as possible who shared their concern, we sent an email to 5,000-plus nurses with a picture of those *Healer's Touch* sculptures. We assured them that DAISY, like us, was alive and well, and affirmed our commitment to nurses.

Nurses talked about the photo for years after the fire. How they shared it with the people in their lives. How it inspired them and gave them hope. Not us, *it*—the photo of the *Healer's Touch*. Which is why in the fall of 2019, we felt the story of the fire and its aftermath was the perfect way to close the first edition of this book and the final chapter on twenty years of DAISY. Just as we found strength, solace, and joy in each other in creating DAISY in Patrick's memory, we had found all that and more in the entire DAISY community after our trial by fire. DAISY's "life" continued to breathe life into us. We faced the future with optimism.

Little did we know then that in a matter of months something far worse than that fire would consume us all, testing every bit of our optimism and the strength of nurses and first responders everywhere—and, for a short while, uniting billions around the world in gratitude for all they do.

DAISY HONOREE STORY

Cindy J. Ovalle Sanchez, RN

TecSalud, San José and Zambrano Hellion Hospitals
Monterrey, Nuevo Leon, Mexico

My 75-year-old husband was hospitalized for two months. When we knew about his disease, the news hit us like a ton of bricks. We were distressed about the situation and his health condition. Now I can say that we are victorious, the storm is over, he is well and only the memory remains as a bitter pill to swallow.

With all the bad and unexpected news, I am very grateful to the nurses who took care of him and the wonderful care he received, especially from nurse Cindy. Her presence with my husband and family was fundamental. She was always happy and positive, inspiring joy and trying to cheer my husband up. She would play music she liked and figuratively "dance" with him; she would take his hands and move them to the music, making him feel the rhythm.

On Father's Day, she gave me the idea to celebrate it there and texted me to ask me to send her some pictures of my husband with our children. To our surprise, she printed them out and put them on a corkboard with a "Congratulations, Dad!" sign. It was a very touching moment.

She is truly a great human being. She is warm, cheerful, empathetic, positive, extremely professional, and always gives the best of herself for her patients and families. Because of people like her, patients feel welcomed, comforted, accompanied, and never alone.

The best way I can describe what the DAISY Award did for me is to picture a full cup of water. Every time you care for a patient, you pour a little bit out of your cup into theirs. Every time I received a DAISY nomination. it felt as though someone was pouring back into my cup, and when I received the DAISY Award it felt like my cup was overflowing.

Noah Barton MSN, BS, RN

A World of Gratitude

Friday, March 27, 2020. New York City, 7:00 p.m. With most of the United States and increasingly the world locked down in the early days of the COVID-19 global pandemic, the sound of the city's residents banging pots and pans reverberated through the mostly empty streets. People stretched from open windows, stood on terraces and fire escapes, and leaned over rooftops to bang or simply clap and cheer—united not in protest but in gratitude for the city's first responders: the essential and emergency workers, doctors, and nurses on the front lines of the fight against the new and deadly virus we were just beginning to experience and understand. For two minutes straight, the people of New York transformed the otherwise unbearable cacophony of clanging kitchenware into a harmonious salute to the selflessness and sacrifice of the people risking their lives to save others.

As the numbers of people infected, hospitalized, and taken from us by COVID-19 continued to climb, so did the number of people banging and cheering, not just in New York City but around the world. Their gratitude also resounded on countless signs in the windows of buildings and houses, on lawns, in videos and ads, and posts on social media—all broadcasting their love and support for our "heroes" on the front lines. Meals and gift cards arrived *en masse* at hospitals. Donations flowed.

We listened and watched as the world echoed DAISY's message to nurses: *Thank you.*

❀ ❀ ❀

We were on vacation in Australia and New Zealand in January 2020 to relax and refresh after celebrating DAISY's twentieth anniversary when we first heard talk of an unknown and unnamed virus spreading through China. Like so many people, we paid it no mind. Nor did we think much about it when what was now called the novel coronavirus 2019-nCoV had spread to multiple countries, including the United States. (The first case in the U.S. was reported in Seattle, DAISY's birthplace.) But cases overall were still in the single digits, and our excitement for starting DAISY's twenty-first year was growing.

Three nurses—Susan Grant (then CNE at Michigan's Beaumont Health), Cindy Sweeney (DAISY's vice president for nursing), and Melissa Foreman-Lovell (then CNO at Beaumont Hospital—Royal Oak) had just published their 2019 pilot study in *Nurse Leader* (see page 142) on what it meant to patients and families to say thank you to their nurses by writing a DAISY nomination. "Expressing Gratitude: Findings from Patients and Families Who Nominate Nurses for The

DAISY Award" examined nominations from four Beaumont hospitals in Michigan, and their key points reinforced more than ever the importance of meaningful recognition to patients and families. The study's conclusion said it all: "Providing the means to express gratitude and capture the patient–family voice should be a priority for health care leaders to initiate and sustain." Simply put, patients and nurses needed DAISY, and we were ready to get back on the road and continue to sustain its success, starting with the publication of the first edition of this book.

We received the first copies of our book around the same time the pilot study was published and did some local launch events to prepare for our first big book signing at the American Organization for Nursing Leadership (AONL) conference in March. Peak promotion and a book tour were scheduled during Nurses' Week in May and would continue throughout 2020.

Then AONL canceled. Then everything shut down. As the world banged and proclaimed their gratitude to everyone on the front lines of the pandemic, we were suddenly struck silent. The irony was not lost on us. While seemingly everyone was recognizing nurses as part of their salutes, we had to figure out how to keep DAISY recognition going—how to keep shining the light through the darkest time most nurses had ever known.

❋ ❋ ❋

What DAISY was going through was not unique. We were asking the same question every business and every person was that March: *What do we do now?* But our "customers" and the people we served were on the front lines of the battle, not stuck at home like the rest of us. Contactless delivery, six feet of separation, and masks couldn't get us outside to celebrate, and no one was going inside a hospital unless they had to. On the one hand, we wanted to keep recognition going. On the other hand, the last thing we wanted was to make recognition an added source of work stress for our partners. Few nursing leaders were thinking about presenting awards in those early months, and we knew how nurses and all first responders felt: exhausted, stressed, and overwhelmed.

So: What could we do for them?

The first thing we did was practice the very thing DAISY recognizes: kindness and compassion. As vice president of operations, Melissa led the team through softening our email requests, knowing how busy DAISY coordinators were. Messages we left for them were filled with positivity and encouragement. We made sure they knew we were here if they needed us. That we would do anything we could to help when they were ready. If we didn't hear back, we did not hound them. But we did hear back from many coordinators at even the busiest hospitals, who thanked us for our support. They still wanted to recognize their nurses but were—unsurprisingly—way behind. What we heard next from many of them was devastating.

"People would burst into tears during calls, talking about the suffering and death around them," Melissa recalls. "Nurses would tell us stories of being with a patient in one bed as they passed away and then

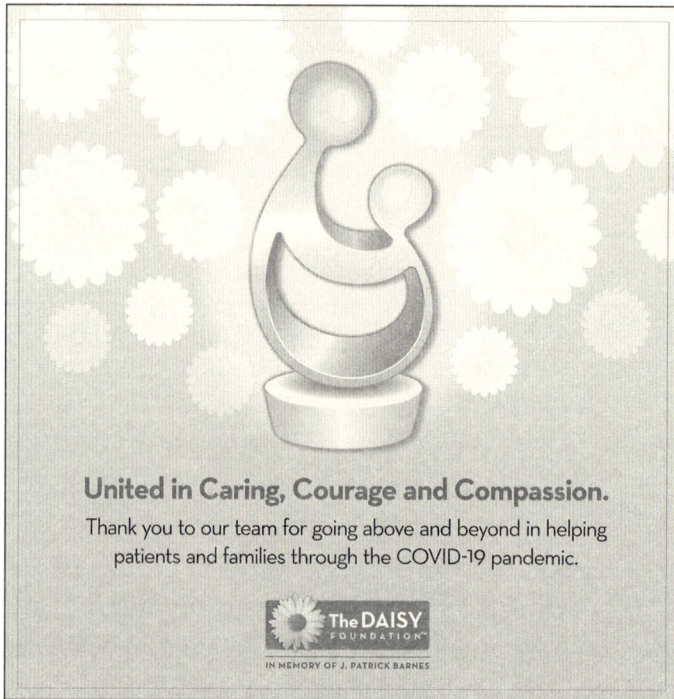

DAISY's "United in Caring" Banner

having to move to the bed next to that one to be with another patient as they died. There was no downtime. No time to process and deal with their own grief. They tried to reach out to families, holding phones to the ears of loved ones to make each passing less lonely for the patients and the families who could not be by their sides."

Getting this glimpse into what nurses were going through was a heartbreaking privilege we did not take lightly. We needed to do something different—something more than just adapt our nurse recognition program to the times. DAISY was about recognizing nurses, but our partners needed ways to thank not just nurses but everyone serving on the front lines. Everyone on the DAISY team agreed we had to echo and amplify those pots and pans to recognize everyone who was risking their lives to help and save others. But how?

What Bonnie came up with, and Melissa and the team made a reality that May, was "United in Caring, Courage and Compassion." The program gave hospitals a way to immediately thank everyone for "going above and beyond in helping patients and families through the COVID-19 pandemic." We created a four-foot square "United in Caring" banner with those words and a *Healer's Touch* background. The banner could be signed by all members of a hospital's team. We also made smaller

"United in Caring" Banner signed by the team at
Columbus Regional Health, Columbus, IN, July 2021.

plaques that looked like the banners, as well as United in Caring pins for team members to wear with pride for all they were doing. We offered large *Healer's Touch* sculptures to display in honor of everyone involved in fighting COVID-19.

❀ ❀ ❀

While "United in Caring" allowed our partners to recognize their nurses and teams in a different way, we knew we couldn't lose our focus on the DAISY Awards. Many of our partners understood what the Beaumont study and the rest of the research showed: the importance of gratitude and recognition to nurses and their patients/families. Our partners wanted to keep DAISY going. They were ready to do whatever it would take to recognize individual nurses and nurse-led teams. They had pre-COVID awards to present that the shutdown had put on hold, and new awards to present.

Of course, DAISY was built on celebrating nurses in person, but no one was gathering in hospitals for the foreseeable future. Thank heavens for Zoom. Susan Brown, the chief nursing officer at City of Hope in California, showed us what was possible. When we knew we had to help our partners present their DAISY Awards virtually, she said, "I got this. We're going to do this really well." She more than kept that promise. From almost the start of the shutdown, City of Hope continued to present six awards each quarter. Susan and her team created beautiful and deeply moving PowerPoint presentations that she displayed as she read the Honorees' nomination stories. She augmented them with stories of her own, as she knew all the nurses personally. Hundreds of people attended, including Bonnie and/or someone else from DAISY, so we always had a presence. Our industry partners sat in too, each presentation reminding them of what nurses were going through and why their support for DAISY was so vital.

Susan was an inspiration to us. To help her and to help those partners who needed more support and specifics on how to sustain DAISY in this new world, our team created best practices for presenting virtually. We did everything we could to make the DAISY presentations as easy as possible and help ensure they happened, and our weeks were soon full of calls and award presentations. We coached coordinators on how to do DAISY without gathering in person and promised someone from our team would be there every step of the way and attend whenever possible to make them extra special. We created celebration packets. We made sure the awards were sent to the Honorees' homes, not the hospitals. (We later generated ideas for in-person presentations when some restrictions were lifted, respecting the need for things like masks and social distancing.) Tena and her marketing team then did a fabulous job getting out the stories we heard to inspire nurses and other partners—to celebrate the positive that nurses were doing, not just depict the exhaustion and mourn the losses.

Nurses were finding their own ways to shine the light on all the right, too. They made sure to wave at the people banging those pots and pans. They lined the walls of their hospitals and cheered as patients who survived were released. They put pictures of themselves on their protective equipment so patients could see the smiling faces behind the masks. Kindness is adaptable, and its evolution was captured in a September 2020 video series created by one of our industry partners, Careismatic Brands. Honoring the world's nurses and sending a message of "love, hope, and profound gratitude," the series kicked off with *In the Year of the Nurse—A Tribute to Courage*. The video is filled with images of nurses on the front lines during COVID while children sing George Harrison's "Give Me Love."

"We see you. We hear you. We sing this song for you." Those were the words the children said to the nurses before they started singing. The words still move us deeply.

A Tribute to Courage has been viewed by more than 4.5 million people—and it raised more than $100,000 for the DAISY Foundation to fund nurse-led research on how to bring high-quality care to underserved communities. It also helped spread the word about DAISY during a time when it was hard for patients to know who we were.

❀ ❀ ❀

While we had succeeded in keeping recognition going, nominations for DAISY Awards were way down. At first that was because families could not be with their loved ones in person for any procedure, let alone with those dealing with COVID-19. They could not meet the nurses and see the compassionate care they were providing. That also meant they could not see the signs and cards about the DAISY Awards and pick up a form to nominate their nurses and show their gratitude. We soon learned that even if they could have been there, there were no forms there for them to fill out.

We have a group of nurses we talk to regularly to ask what is going on and to keep us connected to the work being done. It was clear when we talked to them during COVID that hospitals had disposed of everything on paper. There were no more cards to leave by bedsides, no nomination forms or boxes. Nothing. Most patients and families didn't just submit nominations this way, they learned about DAISY this way! We needed a way for patients and families to come to our website, select their hospital, and nominate their nurse through DAISY. We asked our industry partner and longtime friends at Get Well, a global digital health company, to create a nomination form for every DAISY hospital on DAISYfoundation.org. By the end of 2020, we had links to nomination forms on our website for every DAISY facility, and we emailed them links and QR codes so they could promote DAISY via electronic nominations inside their buildings.

Having the QR code was huge because it allowed us—for the first time—to speak directly to the world. Previously we were limited to the four walls of the hospitals and anything they did inside using the materials we provided them. To help promote this new way to nominate, Mark called on his relationships from his past life in the billboard industry. Their companies gave us space to announce our electronic nominations, including two enormous signs in New York City's Times Square that appeared in January 2021. Tena, too, leveraged her advertising relationships, and together they collected more than $1 million of free billboard space around the country, encouraging the public to say thank you to nurses by nominating them for DAISY Awards.

But while electronic nominations and QR codes for our partners made it much easier for patients and families to recognize nurses, and the billboards drove new awareness outside of hospitals, nominations still weren't flowing in like before. Melissa identified the problem from an operational standpoint.

"When COVID started, there were no family members in hospitals to write the nominations, and patients were too sick to write them," Melissa says. "Often they couldn't find a nomination form even if they wanted to. Many DAISY programs went on hold, and some had to lay off their DAISY coordinators. By the end of 2020 more than 400 new partners had signed on to our program. Yet many hadn't identified coordinators. So all our partners had this electronic nomination form we created for them, but many had no idea that they had it. How do we show all our partners how to collect nominations as easily as possible,

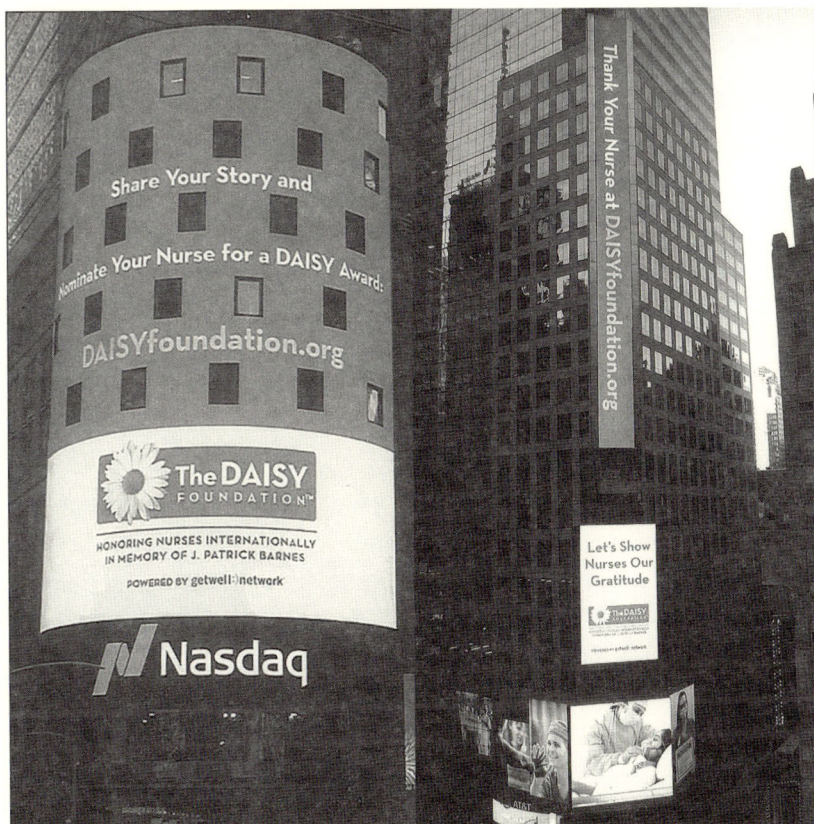

DAISY Nomination Billboards in Times Square, New York City, January 2021

given the lack of time and people that hospitals had to implement DAISY?"

Our team's mantra in 2021: Make sure our partners know what they have, and make DAISY as easy as possible to get going again. Janet Silvestri, our program director for the Midwest, even put together a video on how to use a spreadsheet to track nominations, and to blind nominees' names easily to make sure selection was fair. She and our team then reached out everywhere they could to offer encouragement and help. *You do not have to reprint your forms and put out boxes right now. You don't have to start from scratch. You have this QR code and electronic form to make it easy for yourself and your patients and families!*

The team's efforts paid off—and then some. By the end of 2021, nominations were not just going up; they were poised to exceed our previous annual records. But it wasn't just nominations. It was all things DAISY. The pots and pans may have stopped banging as we came out of the shadow of COVID, but DAISY's world of gratitude was going stronger than ever as we headed into 2022. And as in-person gatherings became a thing of the present, we decided it was time for all of us at DAISY to be part of the celebrations again.

❀ ❀ ❀

We suppose we could have picked somewhere closer than Ireland to travel to for our first post-COVID in-person presentations in June 2022. But the idea of returning to a country we loved and combining it with our annual board meeting was too tempting. We had all our COVID vaccines and boosters. Ireland had lifted all its COVID restrictions. We had fond memories of meeting the country's very first DAISY nurse, Rob Lynch from Mater Misericordiae University Hospital in Dublin, in March 2019, and always wanted to return. Another nurse in Ireland once told us he'd been doing his job for 40 years and never worked a day in his life. Those words had never left us. We felt comfortable and excited to go.

Our Lady of Lourdes Hospital in the town of Drogheda was willing to delay the ceremony for its next DAISY Award to coincide with our visit on June 23rd, and we built our plans around them. It was a beautiful presentation celebrating the honoree, Gillian Browne, and all ten nominees for that quarter. Everyone was masked, but talk of COVID was minimal compared to the importance of DAISY to their nurses and patients and their families.

Feeling great, we headed to Dublin where we were given a tour of the nursing school at the prestigious Royal College of Surgeons in Ireland, which also sponsored the DAISY Award for its hospital group. Our bus driver was a former pub owner who regaled us with fabulous stories. Everything seemed back to normal—only it was the new normal.

After we arrived in Dublin, we learned why the city was so mobbed: that Saturday was Dublin Pride. It was a glorious sea of color and life, but social distancing was impossible. Masks were not anywhere to be found. The first day of our board meeting, Mark woke up with COVID. Then Melissa started coughing and tested positive. Then Bonnie. The three of us attended the board meeting via Zoom, but the rest of the members were there in person and more than socially distant. Some of them still ended up with COVID. Thankfully and gratefully, between our shots, the Paxlovid antiviral pills we had been advised to bring with us, and otherwise good health, it was more annoying than anything else. We refused to let it dim our trip or the board's optimism.

Our first in-person meeting in the United States post-COVID was not until October, at the Hospital of the University of Pennsylvania, Bonnie's undergraduate alma mater. We didn't attend an award presentation, but they had some of their DAISY Honorees, the entire DAISY team, the CNO, and the president of the hospital at the meeting. The hospital understood the importance of recognition and had sustained DAISY throughout COVID. Now they wanted to hear more about best practices to get more nominations. They wanted to make the program even stronger. Their words were echoed at our next meeting, at the Children's Hospital of Philadelphia, where we attended a DAISY Award presentation and heard how important DAISY had been since the pandemic started.

Again and again, in Ireland and Philadelphia and from our partners around the world, the message was clear: Sustaining DAISY gave them a sense of normalcy. We knew then that COVID might always be with us—but so would DAISY.

Were we afraid at times that the global pandemic might bring DAISY down? Absolutely. The World Health Organization estimated that 115,000 healthcare workers died in 2020 because of COVID-19, and the *Guardian* and Kaiser Health News estimated a third of those workers were nurses. Hundreds of thousands more were infected that first year. But while our ability to shine the light on all the right might have flickered, the need to do so never did. Our partners and the nurses themselves understood more than ever the power of gratitude and the importance of recognition. While some programs went on hold, not one left DAISY.

In fact, DAISY *grew* every year from 2019 to 2023, domestically and internationally. Before COVID, we had more than 4,100 partners at healthcare facilities and schools of nursing. At the start of 2024, we had more than 6,500 and many of our partners from pre-2020 have increased their DAISY programs. DAISY is honoring nurses in 41 countries, up from 25 in 2019. Most gratifying was the increase in nominations and awards. At the end of 2019, we had received 1.6 million DAISY Award nominations and honored 136,000 nurses and teams. *At the end of 2023, more than 2.8 million people had written DAISY nominations, and we had honored more than 250,000 nurses, nurse leaders, nurse-led teams, educators, and students.*

Our world of gratitude was growing.

DAISY HONOREE STORY

Lori Tisdale, MSN, RN, CPN, CNE
Charleston Southern University
North Charleston, South Carolina

'll never forget my first day of lecture with Professor Tisdale in Pediatric Nursing. Her passion for ensuring the well-being of others shined through each shared experience during her introductory speech. I learned one thing very quickly: Her abilities go beyond teaching nursing students skills and procedures.

On my first day, Professor Tisdale shared her "why" for choosing nursing as a career, that "why" being her young daughter, who sadly passed away far too soon. She made me start thinking about my "why," my reason for choosing nursing. Those words keep me motivated to this day to treat every patient and family member that I encounter with grace, compassion, and respect. Because that should be every nurse's "why." She challenges nursing students to tackle uncomfortable conversations head-on and to integrate faith into every patient and family interaction; to be the nurses who comfort a child while the parents step out to get morning coffee; to be the nurses to offer parents breaks throughout the day to de-stress; to be the nurses that hold the parents' hands after hearing unexpected news about their child's prognosis. With great confidence, I can say that Professor Tisdale has positively impacted her colleagues and students. We could all benefit from discovering our "why," as Professor Tisdale has.

In the midst of the Great Resignation and unprecedented high compassion fatigue, we were desperate to change the climate. Bringing DAISY to the nurses was just the drop in temperature we were striving for. It brought meaningful recognition and positive energy to our staff, their families, and administrations during a difficult time.

Monica Schafer, CNO

We Are a Bigger Family

In the previous chapter, we said that the first thing we did after the shutdown was practice the very things DAISY recognizes: kindness and compassion. That is true. But we did not start with our partners. How could we understand and show compassion for what nurses were going through if we did not recognize what our people were going through?

Shining the Light on All the Right

We used to say we had two daughters (Tena Barnes Carraher and Melissa Barnes) and a brother (Peter Maher) running DAISY with us. As Patrick's widow, Tena was born into the story of DAISY and now brilliantly leads the marketing and communications team. Peter, who has been with us since 2009, will never be anything but "Benedict" to Mark for continuously supporting Bonnie over him, but his love of DAISY is even greater than his immense skills as our chief financial officer/controller/bookkeeper/human resources director/traitor. And Melissa, who joined us in 2011 when we needed her to help scale DAISY, has done just that as our vice president for all operations.

If it had been just the five of us running DAISY in March 2020, we wouldn't have had to say much to know we were going to be okay. But we had a whole family tree running DAISY when the pandemic started. So with Melissa and Tena we called each team member to make sure that they felt safe, explain that we were not expecting them to do anything that made them feel otherwise, and assure them that their jobs were secure.

"We started by listening to and addressing the fears and uncertainties within our own organization" says Melissa. "We wanted to make sure our team was able to be their compassionate selves without having to worry if our partners couldn't respond or do awards, put their programs on hold, or didn't need anything from DAISY to recognize their nurses. We just focused on showing support and love with zero pressure. That sustained our relationships inside and outside DAISY. Tena became our virtual 'cruise director' and planned online social hours to keep our team connected, playing games like DAISY bingo, organizing virtual scavenger hunts and trivia nights, and having us share our favorite books, recipes, movies, and TV shows. The love and compassion we showed each other allowed DAISY to turn around and show even more compassion to our partners."

✽ ✽ ✽

Mark likes to say that after ten years DAISY was an overnight success. After 25 years, he feels we are an even bigger overnight success, because of our team. Simply put, celebrating the art of nursing around the world needs a team that values nurses and recognition as much as we do. First, they worked with us to pivot how DAISY operated. Then, as the world opened up again, they re-established the programs that had been on hold. Finally, while helping our existing partners, they welcomed thousands of new ones, worldwide, that understood the value of DAISY and the power of recognition.

As our "Queen of Execution," Melissa charted our path through all that craziness of the last five years. "If I have an idea for something like 'United in Caring,' Melissa figures out how it can be done, and she and Tena make it happen with the team," says Bonnie. "They execute 99 of my 100 ideas, and the one they don't was not worth executing anyway."

But it is Melissa's vision for putting our team in the right places, not just her execution, that makes DAISY so strong. As we have grown, so has our leadership team under Melissa. Consider just a few of them and how they have grown since they started: Christina Jairamani and Janet Silvestri, who have been with us for more than ten years, and Alex Schoen, who has been with us since 2017.

Next time you see our graphics, website, and wonderful videos, think of Christina, who was a program coordinator when she joined DAISY but has evolved under Melissa into our self-taught IT director plus creative director. (Her 2024 video explaining the difference between a nominee pin and an honoree pin garnered the biggest viewership of anything we have ever posted on social media—even tens of thousands on TikTok, where we have few followers!) If you are at a DAISY partner in the Midwest, you know Janet's work as the program director, where she supports around 500 healthcare organizations and 70 schools of nursing. And Alex, who directs programs for our international partners, started as a DAISY coordinator at two of our hospitals in Toledo, Ohio.

Overall, we now have a wonderful and dedicated team of 31 people working out of their homes in 11 states, and there isn't anything we can't do to serve our partners. But when Cindy Sweeney, our vice president for nursing, retired in early 2021, we all acknowledged that we lacked something when it came to the profession we recognize: *None of us were nurses.*

Shining the Light on All the Right

DAISY serves nurses and works with nurses every day. We study the nursing profession intensely. But we are entrepreneurs. We are driven by our desire to recognize nurses of all kinds in memory of Patrick, and we value to the deepest level the importance of nurses around the world. We know that nurses offer different perspectives on DAISY, which is why we have had so many nurses on our board to help guide us. But we are not nurses.

DAISY's value and the value of meaningful recognition were now established—in research and in the sheer number of partners we had globally. Our team had proved they could handle anything life threw at us. The question was: *Where could we take DAISY?* Without Cindy, Bonnie didn't have a nurse on the team to bounce new ideas off of about how DAISY could be a part of the larger conversations around nursing, let alone how DAISY could execute them.

We were moving DAISY forward in ways we never could have in our first 20 years, and we needed someone who could be our partner on the inside of the profession. Someone who could sit next to us at the DAISY table and help us know what we still don't know about nurses and nursing. Someone who added immediate value when they joined us at nursing tables as we created and seized opportunities to make DAISY an even bigger partner and presence within the nursing community.

"I wanted a partnership with a nurse leader who could engage ideas intellectually as only a leader of nurses can," Bonnie says. "I wanted someone on the DAISY team who had an intimate understanding of DAISY's mission and vision, and believed as we believe that meaningful recognition can have a more significant influence in healthcare."

Turns out, she was already part of our extended DAISY family.

❋ ❋ ❋

Deb Zimmermann was unfamiliar with the DAISY Foundation in 2009 when she became chief nursing executive at Virginia Commonwealth University (VCU) Health System and the nurses came to her with a request to bring in the DAISY Award program. They thought it would be wonderful to have a mechanism for patients and families to express gratitude to nurses for the difference that they made. The nurses said they would coordinate it; Deb only needed to approve it and participate in the ceremonies.

Deb did not hesitate in saying yes to her nurses. She loved that her clinical nurses approached her with a nonclinical idea, and DAISY's costs were very reasonable. She just didn't know if it would make a difference. She believed that the recognition programs VCU had in place were robust and were recognizing the right things. (Which is why Cindy Lefton later developed a presentation of her research called "Pizza Is Great, But It's Not Meaningful Recognition.")

Deb was of course hardly unique among CNOs, CNEs, and indeed most nurses at the time. Most nurses did not see their care as extraordinary and needing recognition. They said something like "I was only doing my job." Nurses are clinicians. Nursing is a profession based on science and evidence, and in 2009 DAISY did not have the science and evidence to support the power of meaningful recognition and positive feedback from families.

"I had no clue what we were missing at VCU," Deb recalls. "Sometimes because of our education or the focus on clinical care, nurses don't always see how what we used to call 'soft skills' matter as much as the clinical work we do. What I learned from DAISY is that feedback from patients, families, and colleagues filled nurses' cups. It created a culture of kindness, a culture of innovation, a culture of teamwork. And it was magical. DAISY spread like wildfire and impacted not just the nurses but my entire organization."

Deb was excited to tell us the story of that magic when she met us at the Magnet conference later that year. She came to the DAISY booth to tell us how incredible DAISY had been for VCU. How all nurses needed to hear that they were making a difference. How each nomination pierced or prevented that hard shell of cynicism that some nurses develop. How DAISY did what the other recognition programs did not: show them how their skill and compassion had made a difference to the patients and families they served.

"DAISY reminds nurses why they chose to be nurses in the first place," Deb said. "DAISY ties nurses to their purpose."

DAISY ties nurses to their purpose. We had never heard someone say that to us before.

Deb's profound belief in the power of DAISY, her understanding of what makes it successful and different than other forms of recognition in hospitals, and her innate understanding of what makes nurses tick—she's a nurse's nurse and fun to be around—is why we asked her to join our board in 2018.

As we got to know Deb, we learned more about her work as an army nurse, and nurse practitioner, and her other nursing leadership roles. We learned how intimately she believed in DAISY: She hadn't just read thousands of nominations, she has written three of them—not as a nurse but as family of a patient. As a former chair of ANCC's Magnet Commission and candidate for president of AONL, she seemed the perfect nurse for what DAISY needed to help us

The DAISY Leadership Team. Left to right: Mark, Bonnie, Peter, Deb, Tena, and Melissa. ANCC National Magnet/Pathway to Excellence Conference, Philadelphia, 2022.

grow. In November 2021, we asked her to join our immediate family as our CEO.

Team player that she is, when we Zoomed with her to offer her the position, her husband Gary was with her. "We say yes!"

※ ※ ※

After Deb came on board, she quickly learned she should let the DAISY team run DAISY and instead help us avoid mistakes, telling us which ideas were in conflict with or could not work for nurses. But her focus has been on her role as a national nurse leader to help bring greater awareness throughout healthcare of DAISY's mission of shining the light on all the right—how it fits into essential discussions around nurses' well-being, healthy workplace environments, and the future of nursing.

"DAISY is about human connection—what's right and good—and putting together a collaborative environment that benefits everyone," Deb says. "As master conveners and connectors, DAISY can bring together clinicians and patients and communities. We can be a leader in improving the health and wellness of nurses. We can change the narrative around nursing to bring more people into the profession and keep the nurses we already have."

After almost 25 years of recognizing nurses, DAISY was poised to play a bigger part in rewriting the post-COVID story of beleaguered and exhausted nurses by highlighting the positive. Because we're about shining the light on the right.

DAISY HONOREE STORY

Madeline Dexter, BSN, RN
Baystate Medical Center
Springfield, Massachusetts

ER visits are inherently bad. But I am very comfortable saying that this visit was an excellent experience against all odds. We were seen promptly and received the best care possible even when the department was very busy.

We were largely cared for by a nurse named Madeline Dexter. Maddie truly holistically cared for our son, making him feel safe and understood. Maddie was introduced to his precious triceratops stuffie and immediately began including her and referring to her by name, assuring our son that they also specialized in dinosaur care. Regardless of how busy they may have been, Maddie swabbed the dinosaur, checked its vitals, gave the dinosaur medicine, and cared for it just as she did our son. Not only did this make him smile in scary circumstances, but it also made him feel as though what mattered to him also mattered to her—a wonderful place for a feeling of safety for a very scared little boy.

There's something truly heartening about seeing a nurse adorned with a badge full of DAISY pins. It's a visual testament to their dedication and the impact they've made on the lives of others.

Alicia Allen, CNO

Nursing the Power of Recognition

You often hear Oscar nominees who don't win say something like, "I was happy just to be nominated." Some of them even mean it. A DAISY Nominee always does. For millions of nurses, the thank-yous from patients and families for the kindness and compassionate care they showed are meaningful recognition. The nominations are what remind them of why they became nurses and connect them to their purpose. They say, "The awards committee may not have selected me, but my patient did." Take the nurse Deb met when she went in for knee surgery. She proudly wore her five-time-nominee pin and another single nominee pin on her ID badge and could tell Deb the stories of the patients/families behind each nomination. The pins were her "medals," and they reminded her of that connection every day.

Hospitals have increasingly understood the importance of DAISY nominations to nurses, which is why we urge our partners to give nominee pins to all who are nominated and to publicize the nurses who receive them. The pins magnify their cultures of recognition, which is essential to retaining *all* their nurses. After all, the nominee pins don't

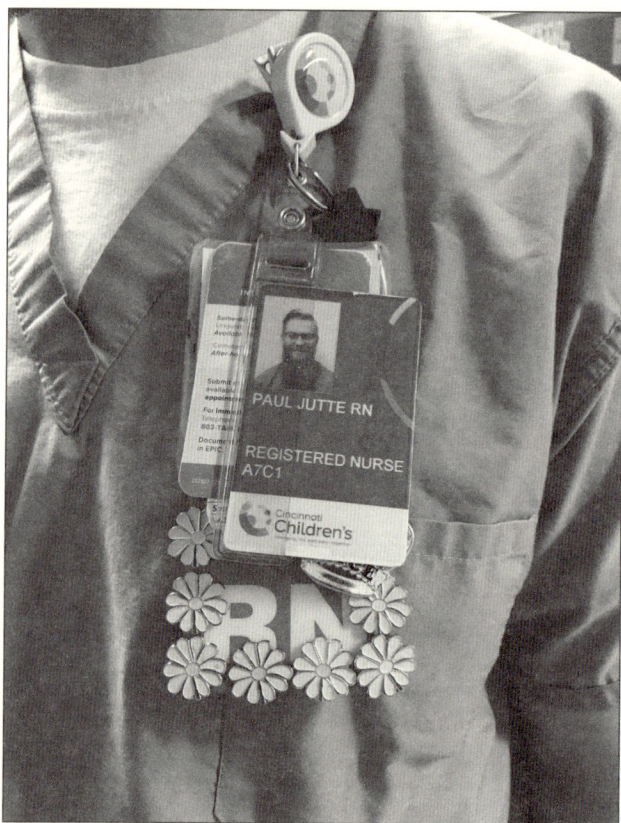

Paul Jutte, RN, Cincinnati Children's Hospital,
proudly displaying his DAISY nominee pins for the DAISY Award

just remind the nurses who wear these pins of their patients and purpose—they remind every nurse who sees those pins, too. Understanding these connections is the biggest reason we've sent out more than 2.8 million nominee pins since they were created in 2006. The only person who doesn't love everything about them is Erin Ascher, our executive assistant, who is tasked with replacing lost ones, and it is hard work to keep up with the requests.

That said, the meaningful recognition that flows through every DAISY nominee pin, award, and the work of the entire foundation is tied to more than connection to purpose for nurses and retention of nurses in hospitals. It is tied to the future of nursing.

※ ※ ※

Simply put, COVID-19 dealt a blow to nursing. First and foremost, tens of thousands of nurses lost their lives through their altruistic tendencies to put themselves and potentially their families at risk while battling an unknown disease. Then came the exodus.

The data on the nursing profession from 2021 and 2022 was bleak. There were 5.2 million registered nurses (RNs) in the United States in 2023 when the National Council of State Boards of Nursing (NCSBN) released "Examining the Impact of the COVID-19 Pandemic on Burnout and Stress Among U.S. Nurses." According to the survey, 100,000 RNs had left the workforce the previous two years due to "stress, burnout, and retirements," and 18 percent of new RNs had quit within their first year. The result was a 2.7 percent decline in RNs (and 3.3 percent of all nurses). More than 15 percent of RNs told NCSBN they intended to leave within five years. Soon after the NCSBN survey was released, the American Association of Colleges of Nursing reported that the number of students entering nursing programs to become RNs declined by 1.4 percent in 2022, ending two decades of enrollment growth.

With retention and recruitment of RNs and all nurses at a premium, meaningful recognition was now an important tool for hospitals and healthcare organizations. Hospital CEOs repeatedly told us we were an essential part of their strategic plans. If research hadn't already quashed any doubts about DAISY's importance to nurses and patients/

families and demonstrated that DAISY could change the culture of an organization, the evidence following COVID did: Data showed that organizations that had continued to recognize their nurses during the pandemic had lower turnover rates since COVID began, partly because they continued to focus on the right.

The idea that anyone needed a pandemic, research, or permission to celebrate the compassionate care that nurses deliver and how meaningful recognition makes you feel still drives Mark crazy sometimes. (Okay, all the time.) But it bears repeating that this increased acceptance of and demand for DAISY is a major shift for nurses and nursing.

Nurses have always chosen to be nurses for the impact they can have on others and to make the health and wellness of their communities better. But as experience and every nurse who has been a part of DAISY's family have taught us, nursing is a profession of science. Nurses are clinicians and learn to focus on the problems. They haven't been taught that positive feedback through meaningful recognition from patients matters, so they don't think about its importance.

We have always been told that nurses are trained to look for what's wrong. As Deb says, "Nurses are taught five different ways to ask a patient about their pain, or to get to the source of a problem. A clinical approach to our work is essential, but it has a negative effect on us even if it is positive to the patient. Nurses also have fought to be recognized as partners with doctors and other medical colleagues. In the past, they had a perception that recognizing and celebrating 'soft skills' like compassion diminished them as clinicians. So, many nurses dismissed soft skills as 'just doing my job.'"

Not anymore. Today, millions of nurses know how positive feedback and meaningful recognition for those "soft skills" through DAISY fills you up—what Cindy Lefton calls "compassion satisfaction"—and how to accept that recognition as a gift. DAISY compels them to look at the positive and understand that there is the need to receive more than data. They feel how being recognized keeps them going on difficult days, and creates a cycle of gratitude and kindness. That cycle has even widened to their seizing the opportunity to recognize each other.

Perhaps the most gratifying part of the massive increase in DAISY nominations since COVID is the fact that *nurses* are nominating other nurses for DAISY Awards. It's exciting to see them so inspired by the stories of care they hear that they write a nomination for another nurse to show the power of recognition to their colleagues. They are learning that it is just as therapeutic for them as it is for patients and families to say thank you. And a nurse who gets nominated by another nurse feels seen in a way that binds them to the profession and each other.

To make sure DAISY can recognize as many of these nurses as possible wherever they practice, wherever they are in their careers, we keep expanding how the awards flow through every part of the profession. Since our 20th anniversary, we have added a DAISY Award for ethics, and in response to George Floyd's murder and the immediate awareness of the health inequities in our society, an additional award for

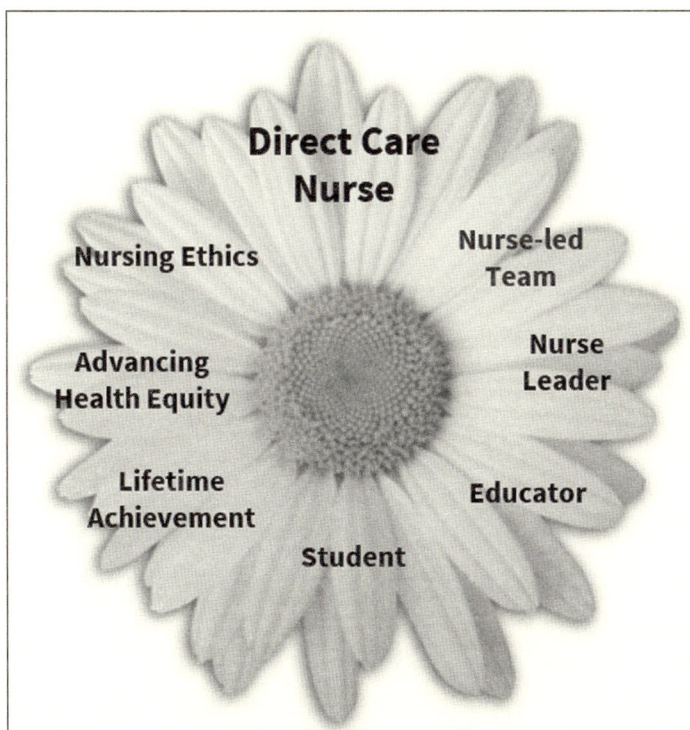

Honoring nurses wherever they practice, wherever they are in their careers

advancing health equity, for a total of eight. We also collaborate with other organizations on international awards, such as with the Institute for Healthcare Improvement (IHI) for patient and workforce safety, with HealthImpact for policy that advances compassionate care, and with the American Nurses Association (ANA) for ethics in practice and leadership. This evolution of our program awards, like the elevation of DAISY nominations among nurses, was not part of our original strategic plan, but they are the cornerstones we are building on for the future.

※ ※ ※

Enough of the pictures of the beleaguered and exhausted nurses! These are the words the renowned Dr. Peter I. Buerhaus spoke just a few years after we started DAISY. Peter is a nurse and a healthcare economist who was studying nursing and physician workforces at the start of the 21st century when he observed the ongoing decline in nursing school enrollments. He predicted a huge nursing shortage if it continued. So he set out to change the trajectory.

Peter saw a causal link between the negative public press around nurses and the decline in enrollments. They were portrayed as beleaguered and exhausted. Stories and TV shows played up the friction between them and hospital leadership, and the idea that they lacked status in the continuum of care. To address this negativity, Peter approached Johnson & Johnson, and they collaborated on the "Campaign for Nursing's Future."

Backed by tens of millions of dollars from the pharmaceutical and healthcare giant, the multilayered public policy, advertising, and marketing campaign was launched in 2003. Peter helped guide it to portray nursing the way DAISY was just beginning to: by shining a light on the right to raise national awareness of the importance of the nursing profession, increase and promote the image of nurses, and encourage people to become RNs.

The Campaign for Nursing's Future produced national television commercials showcasing nurses and their importance to healthcare delivery and patients. It highlighted nurses' strength, compassion, and expertise and showed how they make a difference to and raise up the health and wellness of the country. It created a website and printed materials promoting nursing careers to high school and college guidance and career counselors. It organized large-scale celebrations of nurses throughout the country to raise awareness of the nursing profession and to raise funds to support students and faculty. The impact of all that and more was immediate and lasting in preventing a national nursing shortage: Enrollment at nursing schools increased in the campaign's first year and every year until it ended in 2023—just when enrollments declined and the nation faced a nursing shortage again.

So we all wondered: Could DAISY be a part of helping those numbers rebound, and honor the legacy of the Campaign for Nursing's Future?

❀ ❀ ❀

DAISY already had success working with AONL on a new program to increase recognition around nurse leaders and COVID-19. In July 2020, AONL and Joslin Insight, a healthcare market research firm, did their first survey in a longitudinal study of the impact of the pandemic on nurse leaders' well-being and on the new challenges they faced. That survey and each subsequent one showed the importance of recognition to nurse leaders. In a list of advancements that nurse leaders wanted to see sustained after the pandemic, only the increased use of telehealth topped an expansion of recognition for the value that nurse leaders provide.

In the section "A Day in the Life of a Nurse Leader," awards and recognition were just behind employee engagement/retention on the list of tasks that brought them the most joy and caused them almost no frustration.

Daryl Joslin told Bonnie what the data revealed, and Bonnie called Deb, who was on the boards of both DAISY and AONL at the time. "Nurse managers are asking for recognition, but we know they will never ask for it for themselves," Bonnie told Deb. "Could we work on addressing this study together? We can take care of elevating the recognition of nurse managers and other leaders while AONL takes care of the other things those leaders need."

We ended up with a two-pronged approach. AONL led a workforce committee focused on redesigning the role of nurse managers, how to support them, and the effectiveness of new models of care. DAISY partnered with AONL and designed an initiative we called "Beyond Gratitude: A Tribute to Nurse Managers" and brought in two of our industry partners, Careismatic Brands and symplr, to fund and amplify it. The tag line echoed the line from the children in Careismatic's video *In the Year of the Nurse—A Tribute to Courage*: "We Hear You. We See You. We Thank You."

The first phase of the campaign launched in 2022 and provided materials like thank-you cards and emails for organizations to express their gratitude to nurse managers. It emphasized the value of adding nurse leader recognition to organizations' DAISY Award regimens. The next phases focused on redesigning nurse managers' work and studying nurse manager recognition. In the first two months, we increased nurse manager recognition by 80 percent.

Then in 2023, with Deb now on our team and the president-elect of AONL, we started to work within the nursing profession. Our goal was to collaborate with healthcare organizations and communities to highlight the exceptional and vital role that nurses play in both of them. We believed in the power of meaningful recognition to help boost retention and recruitment by reminding nurses of their importance to their patients and communities. Healthcare is very local, and DAISY was in practically every community in the United States. We had the trust of nurses. If we could leverage that trust through new partnerships, we could help our partners better connect with their communities about all the right nurses are doing, further spread the importance of compassionate care and recognition, and help lead a change in the public narrative around nursing.

Peter Buerhaus agreed. Bonnie and Deb heard him speak as he neared retirement, in which he laid out his challenges to nursing. Peter did not hold back. He said that the messaging around nursing was again too negative, and that while there were similarities to what occurred 20 years before, the consequences this time could even be worse because of what COVID had wrought. We agreed. Nurses were fed up with the stress in their jobs. Could DAISY and the power of recognition play a part in changing that?

Peter's challenge on messaging was, to us, a call to action: How does DAISY help change the narrative with the public and future nurses?

That question informs pretty much every discussion we have today. It may have taken research, the legacy of a global pandemic, and science-based books like *Compassionomics* and *Wonder Drug: 7 Scientifically Proven Ways That Serving Others Is the Best Medicine for Yourself* to show the importance of meaningful recognition, and how focusing on others helps one find meaning and connection and live a longer, healthier life, but we are gratified to help drive that change for the future.

All this has energized us and our team. We don't talk about retirement. We're having way too much fun forging DAISY's future.

We are continuing our existing partnerships, enhancing and expanding our international partnerships, and forging new partnerships across the continuum of care—such as with nonacute long-term care facilities—to make sure DAISY is honoring nurses wherever they practice. We are partnering with AARP; we hope that exposing their membership to what nursing is all about will encourage them to nominate their nurses for the DAISY Award. And we are honored to have been asked to help create the next generation of nurses: Chamberlain University, the largest school of nursing in the United States and our founding educational partner, is developing a course on compassion in nursing, using a version of this book to reinforce the message.

What will be the future of these initiatives and others to come? Time will tell. But there is only one thing we are certain of: Every time a nurse shows compassion for a patient—whether by taking the temperature of a stuffed dinosaur to make a little boy's care easier, arranging for a terminal patient to see her horse one last time, or just "doing their job"—DAISY will be there to help patients, families, nurses, and anyone else we can say "thank you." Our purpose will always be Patrick.

All we wanted to do was say thank you—then, now, and always.

Shining the Light on People Who Have Helped Make DAISY Right

Twenty-Five Years of Gratitude

Creating this book has been a remarkable process, taking us back in time and reflecting on the many, many people, especially the nurses, who came into our lives and guided us on our DAISY journey.

In 2019, when we first approached Jim Eber, our not-so-ghostlike writer, about working on this project, he told us we were not ready for him yet. We needed to visualize the book—to be clear why we were doing it and know what our message would be. He asked us to spend a little more time thinking about some questions he gave us and then call him again. That conversation was inspirational! Bonnie started writing answers to his questions, and a few weeks later, Jim enthusiastically agreed it was time for us to get to work. He visited us in Glen Ellen, talked with us on the phone, and pored over decades of DAISY's work with us, capturing our stories along with our tears, our laughter, and our efforts to remember things that happened long ago. He spoke to the people who started this journey with us to find out what he—and we—did not know or remember. And then he created this book, which we believe speaks with our voice and DAISY's voice.

As our 25th anniversary approached, we reached out to Jim, who was no less enthusiastic about updating the book to cover the changes and complexities that affected—and continue to affect—healthcare and DAISY. Jim, you have our heartfelt gratitude for sharing this journey with us and for making it so much fun. You and our team of publishing experts—Suzanne Fass of Epstein and Fass Associates, Karen Billipp of Eliot House Productions, and Jane Majkiewicz—have brought this book to life. Special thanks too to Lisa Peterson for holding our hands through this edition's publishing process and to Romana Bova for her beautiful cover design.

What joy we have had reflecting on the last 25 years, going through the DAISY Museum for the first edition in California and for the second edition in our new home in Washington. It is filled with the many gifts nurses and organizations have given us: stuffed animals, elaborate floral displays (now dried), Arabian boxes, porcelain cups, plaques, stunning glass awards, recognitions of DAISY from nursing's professional organizations . . . there's even a wonderful handmade Raggedy Ann. We continue to be struck by just how many people and places fill our hearts. We could not possibly start to recount them all here or we'd have to print another book!

So where *do* we start to acknowledge some of the millions of people—yes, millions if you count all DAISY Nominees and the people who wrote their nominations—who have made DAISY *DAISY* over the last two and a half decades? We start at the beginning. (Note: to make reading the names easier, we have left out all credentials, titles, and ranks; to avoid any sense of favoritism, we have put lists of names in alphabetical order.)

❁ ❁ ❁

To Patrick's nurses: Your compassionate and skillful care for him and us is the reason there is a DAISY Award. We lament that we, like so many people for whom you care, left the hospital without saying a proper thank-you. We simply had to go once we said our last goodbye to him. But our gratitude to you all throughout those weeks, right up to the time you walked us to the door one last time, was immense and has only grown. No words will ever be able to express our appreciation. To Karen Bidwell, Ann Blake, Andi Bowen, Patti Daraskavich, Susan Polizzi Dowling, Debra Goff, Andrea Hanses, Peggy Haug, Tana Irish, Ken Kanfoush, Karen Kuster, Diane Lynn, Lynn Maleta, Vivian Markle, Juanita Merriweather, Terrie Paine, Susan Pambianco, Peggy Stufflebeam, Debra Thomas, Jocelyne Wahl, Robert Young, and any others we missed, thank you. We hope we have done you proud with the DAISY work you inspired.

❁ ❁ ❁

To our family: Our love and respect for nurses is one of so many things we have in common in keeping Pat's spirit alive and present. The loss of Patrick was your loss, too, of course. Thank you for standing by our sides through all these years.

Tena Barnes Carraher, you have been there since the beginning. You have served as a board member and now staff. You combine tremendous creativity and cleverness with a heart of gold and bring it all to DAISY.

Melissa Barnes, we are blessed to have your dedication and operations expertise. Thank you for letting us call you Auntie Bonkers in this book. We all know why we do!

Adam Barnes, we would be buried in legal fees without you and your wise, reasonable, calm counsel.

Brad and Danna Barnes, you have participated in DAISY celebrations and introduced us to the hospital where Danna's dad was a physician.

Wayne, Shelley, Brandon, and Remy Baruch, you have listened to more stories of our DAISY adventures than anyone should have to—Wayne especially, as he has produced the Magnet conference for many years, including the spectacular tribute to DAISY's first 20 years in 2019.

Dave and Marilyn Lauer, you may be gone but we remain forever grateful for your serving on our board and helping facilitate DAISY presentations at our first hospital.

Alexander Barnes, Kate Carraher, and Lauren Carraher, we are so happy that you engage with DAISY as you do. The time, thought, and care you put into reviewing and posting DAISY Honoree nomination stories for our website is oh so appreciated!

Riley Barnes Carraher, we are so proud you! Your dedication to DAISY combined with your love for travel has been a gift. The nurses you met when we toured DAISY hospitals loved meeting Patrick's baby. You provided invaluable support to us during our first International DAISY Day conference in Abu Dhabi. Now that you are an occupational therapist and newly married, we have a wonderful new reply to nurses who ask us how you are doing.

Finally, Dianne Barnes. When she passed away in January 2024, our DAISY family lost a founding member. Dianne helped facilitate our first presentations and then became so much more to DAISY. When we started using SalesForce as our database, Dianne made it the glue that bonded our program team with our healthcare partners. Her mantra was "If it's not in SalesForce, it didn't happen" (a mantra our team still quotes today). It was Dianne who first recognized the power of the nomination stories of DAISY Honorees and insisted we make them public and accessible on our website. She called them "spotlights," and we feature more than 100,000 of them today. We access them and share them constantly, as we do in this book, which means her spirit lives on here and in them.

❀ ❀ ❀

To the nurse leaders who have served on our board of directors: When we created the DAISY Award, we did it out of our need to say thank you to nurses. It didn't occur to us that nurses might benefit from this statement of gratitude. Several nurse leaders—pioneers in partnering with us—saw the value of recognizing compassionate care and the merit and strategic value of our mission. They joined our board and have been holding our hands ever since: Cindy Angiulo, Sheila Antrum, Cynthia Barginere, Karen Cox, Ric Cuming, Stuart Downs, Ann Evans, Kathy Gorman, Susan Grant, Mary Dee Hacker, Beth Heyman, Jane Kamstra, Karlene Kerfoot, and Deb Zimmermann. Where would we be without all of you?

To the "non-nurses" who have served on our board over the years: You did more than provide us with excellent counsel. You believed in our mission, and in some cases even introduced us to hospitals. Norman Cohen, Jennifer Dempsey, the late Lynne Doll, Judy and the late Bruce England, Mark Kamstra, Bonnie Lasky, Julie Moretz, Michael O'Neil, Mike Patterson, and Gayle and John Schofield, thank you from the bottom of our hearts. Special thanks to Daryl Joslin: Your marketing work for API Healthcare impressed us so much that when you left, we asked you to consult with DAISY. Thank you for being a trusted advisor and board member, not to mention a great friend, eating and drinking DAISY every day with us!

To the thousands of other nurse leaders who have impacted us and whose wisdom has guided us: This book's first edition endeavored to thank you all by name. As soon as the book went to press, we realized how many people we had missed, and felt terrible. Now the list is even longer and growing globally every day. To ensure we leave no one out this time, we are sending out a global thank-you. We hope you all know who you are, because we could not be more grateful. You have been an essential part of DAISY.

❋ ❋ ❋

To our team present and past: A simple thank-you seems insufficient. There is no way to adequately express our gratitude for you and your contributions.

Rebecca Blay in Oklahoma, Chelsea Moise in Washington, Janet Silvestri in Michigan, and Alex Schoen in Ohio: As program directors, you represent DAISY with elegance and expertise. You started out as specialists and have taken on additional areas of responsibility with joy, growing into senior roles and teaching our partners the many aspects of DAISY Award implementation that make the program robust in your regions. Special shout-out to Janet, who has been with us for more than ten years and has become a mentor to the rest of the team—and who never forgets to remind us of everyone's birthday and work anniversary.

Vernita Boswell in Indiana, Nicole Dodson in California, Lauren Hairston in Virginia, Ashley Ingram in North Carolina, Jenn Ripley in Texas, Alisha Rowe in Nebraska, Jaci Parks in Ohio, and London Simms in North Carolina: As program managers, your depth of understanding of our mission came quickly and successfully. Your presence and passion for DAISY's mission is contagious!

Kate Ananson in Washington, Amy Ciriot in Texas, Dawn Filipovitch in Ohio, and Lindsey Lawson in Oklahoma: As program specialists, you are linchpins of our communication to our DAISY community far and wide. Your management of SalesForce ensures that everyone on our team knows everything there is to know about every DAISY partner. You share an enthusiasm for our mission and attention to detail that ensures we provide the level of service nurses deserve from us.

Erin Ascher in California: You joined us as an administrative assistant and have become so much more. When we lived in California, you also ran our home and cared for our two German shepherds, Max and Schultz, when we traveled. Now that we live in Washington, you fly or drive to pitch in when we need help, along with the wonderful Brittany "Stardust" Dussault, who lives nearby. You bring laughter and joy to our lives every day. We are so lucky that you are there with us and for us. Always.

Laura Woodward in Washington: You manage our complex calendars, our numerous visits to DAISY partners, our conference plans, our lives, and you make it all look easy. Thank you for tending to DAISY details with joy at every request.

Jennifer Baldwin in California: We would be bankrupt without you as our meticulous and always cheerful bookkeeper, sending out thousands of invoices for everything from annual programs to a small bag of nominee pins. When your workload becomes overwhelming or you take a well-deserved break, Yvonne O'Leary in Washington, formerly our full-time bookkeeper, is ready to step in without missing a step.

Kara Ellis in Oklahoma: Your growth from program specialist to a program director and now marketing manager has been a joy to behold. Thanks to your hard work, DAISY's social media presence is followed by many tens of thousands of nurses and others who love seeing the pictures and news you post every day.

Christina Jairamani in Washington: What other organization has a team member who is both IT director *and* creative director?! Your skills and talent have earned you the name "Her Brilliancy." You taught yourself technology, and your innate design vision has advanced DAISY's branding beautifully. You take the initiative, and everything you touch is better than it was before you touched it.

Dana Love in Washington: How do you do the job of editing the tens of thousands of DAISY Honorees' stories that are registered with us, uploading them to our website, ensuring they're clear of privacy violations, and sharing them with our team, telling us which ones are the "Kleenex alerts" before we read them?!

Peter "Benedict" Maher in California: You are CFO extraordinaire and friend extraordinaire, not to mention the best iPhone photographer of nurses and us ever. Thank you too for bringing your son Luke to our finance team. We will miss him when he graduates from college.

John Reynolds, Manuel Lopez, and Reid Reynolds in California: Where would DAISY be without you? John, our shipping manager since 2009, handles the shipping of every Award and large Healer's Touch from a warehouse that is four times as big as it was pre-COVID. You and your team ensure every box of DAISY gifts and every DAISY display that goes to the numerous conferences we attend is lovingly and meticulously packed—and you somehow send everyone whatever they need on the day they're ordered and paid for. Your dedication is a sight to behold!

Faith Thomas in Washington: As our grants specialist, you beautifully manage a myriad of details with accuracy and commitment to serving applicants and grantees alike.

Deb Zimmermann in Virginia: You joined our board when you were chief nurse executive of an outstanding DAISY health system. Your enthusiasm, your understanding of our program's impact, your insight, your leadership were so strong on the board that when we realized it was time for DAISY to have CEO outside our family, we asked you to take the role. Despite your having just been elected president of the American Organization for Nursing Leadership, you leapt at the opportunity. Your influence on our mission and your widely heard voice have made a difference from day one. We are so happy that DAISY is bringing you joy as together we elevate nurses' visibility and their meaningful recognition.

To those who have come and gone—Kathy Blount, Carol Bramlett, Amanda Dito, Lisa Flaherty, Peggy Gojcaj, Meaghan Kapinos, Elysse Lane, Keisha Mwanganga, Kami Otis, Nan Roderick, Sheri Scholz, and Amy Vetter: Your contributions when you were with us were significant. Julie Blonk, after 12 years with DAISY, we know your decision to leave was a tough one. We will always consider you part of our DAISY family.

Finally, Cindy Sweeney in Maryland: You truly amplified DAISY's voice and visibility with your presentations on DAISY's behalf at nursing conferences, thoughtful articles on meaningful recognition including a column twice a year for the *Journal of Nursing Administration*, and more. You translated the language of nursing for all of us at DAISY. Thank you for being DAISY's Nurse and one of the world's great connectors of people.

❀ ❀ ❀

To our DAISY Supportive Associations: We owe you so much for spreading awareness and increasing the visibility of our work throughout the nursing profession, inviting us to bring DAISY to your conferences and to write for your journals.

The American Organization for Nursing Leadership (AONL) was first, when it was called AONE. In addition to Pam Thompson, whose impact on DAISY is described in this book, we send our gratitude to Robyn Begley, Stacey Chappell, Sue Gergely, Beverly Hancock, MT Meadows, Kourtney Sprout, Angela Taylor, Terese Thrall, Dani Ward, and the numerous AONL board presidents who have embraced us: Rhonda Anderson, Linda Burnes-Bolton, Carol Bradley, Ann Marie Brooks, Laura Caramanica, Bob Dent, Linda Everett, Mary Ann Fuchs, Donna Herrick, Donna Herrin-Griffith, Cheryl Hoying, Michelle Janney, Lois Kercher, Mary Beth Kingston, Linda Knodel, Erik Martin, Pam Rudisill, Kathleen Sanford, Maureen Swick, and Carol Watson.

The American Nurses Credentialing Center (ANCC) came next, bringing the DAISY Award to Magnet-designated organizations and then their Pathway to Excellence program. You welcome us to have annual DAISY Breakfasts for our Magnet partners and for our Pathway to Excellence partners. Each breakfast gives us a platform to share a story of extraordinary nursing. Thank you to every ANCC board and staff member, past and current, who has embraced our work, especially Rhonda Anderson, Loressa Cole, Maricon Dans, Jeff Doucette, Karen Drenkard, Michael Evans, Jeanne Floyd, Ernest Grant, Rebecca Graystone, Debbie Hatmaker, Marianne Horahan, Leigh Hume, Ellen "Boo" Lahman, Maureen Lal, Linda Lewis, Graham Long, Lynn Newberry, Christine Pabico, Pat Reid-Ponte, Liz Stokes, Gregg Tabachow, Tony Ward, Marla Weston, and Laura Wood.

To the American Association of Critical-Care Nurses (AACN): Thank you for your foundational work on meaningful recognition in nursing and for selecting us to receive your esteemed Pioneering Spirit Award at your annual NTI (National Teaching Institute) conference in 2012. We have had a wonderful relationship ever since, thanks to the friendship of Connie Barden, Randy Bauler, Melinda Beckett-Maines, Linda Cassidy, Dorrie Fontaine, Vicki Good, Wanda Johansson, Ramon Lavandero, Dana Woods, and so many members of AACN's board of directors over the years.

To the American Academy of Nursing: We were blown away when you inducted us as honorary fellows in 2012, thereby adding the credential FAAN to our names. Receiving this recognition on behalf of DAISY was unforgettable as Joanne Disch and Diana Mason honored us onstage and the audience stood to applaud our impact. Our sponsors for this surprise recognition were Mary Dee Hacker, Ruth Lindquist, and Roy Simpson. We truly have no words to describe our gratitude to you and the Academy for adding so much credibility and visibility to our work. Thank you too to past president Ken White for adding a "cherry on top" with the Academy's Outstanding Leadership Award!

To Sigma Theta Tau International Honor Society of Nursing: You inducted us as honorary members in 2015 and celebrated DAISY with your Archon Award in 2019. We wear our Sigma pins proudly at all things DAISY, thanks to Ken Dion, Cindy Sweeney, Benson Wright, and others who supported us. Sigma's team of Chris Beaman, Kathy Bennison, Sandra Bibb, Cathy Catrambone, Sarah Gray, Hester Klopper, Liz Madigan, Juli Maxworthy, Richard Ricciardi, Pat Thompson, and Beth Tigges were and are wonderful partners in driving meaningful recognition for nurses.

To the American Association of Colleges of Nursing (AACN): Your guidance and awareness building have been so valuable for the DAISY Faculty Award, which evolved in 2024 to the more inclusive DAISY Award for Nurse Educators. Robert Rosseter, Deb Trautman, and AACN board members: Thank you for issuing national calls to action for educator recognition!

To the American Academy of Ambulatory Care Nurses: When we determined the importance of rolling DAISY across the continuum of care, you were right there to help build awareness of our evolving mission of gratitude to nurses. Thank you, Deena Gilland, Tom Greene, Pete Pomilion, and Jennifer Stranix!

To Janice Brewington, Beverly Malone, Kathleen Poindexter, and Patricia Sharpnack at the National League for Nursing, and to Donna Meyer and Rick Garcia at the Organization of Associate Degree Nursing: You have supported the importance of recognition for educators, as have numerous deans and faculty members who have befriended us and stood up for our mission, including Sharon Goldfarb, Cindy Greenberg, Susan Groenwald, Patty Hurn, Debra Jones, Victoria Rich, Anna Valdez, Ken White, Pat Yoder-Wise, and so many more.

To Melissa Fitzpatrick, then at Hill-Rom, and Patricia McGaffigan, at what is now the Institute for Healthcare Improvement (IHI): You asked what we could do to showcase the important role that nurses play in patient safety, and together we created the DAISY Award for Extraordinary Nurses in Patient Safety. When Baxter acquired Hill-Rom, they sustained their corporate sponsorship for this award that began at its inception. We are grateful that our partnership with IHI is going strong today through Patricia, Jessica Behrhorst, Lindsay Charles-Pierre, Kristin Cronin, and Kedar Mate.

To the Wisconsin League for Nursing: You pointed out to us that there was a gap in our recognition program, overlooking the role of clinical educators in healthcare facilities. These educators help ensure nurses provide care that is evidence based and high quality. You were right. Not only was there nothing DAISY that really pertained to clinical educators, but there was no appropriate recognition for preceptors and mentors. You piloted the concept of the DAISY Award for Extraordinary Nurse Educators that evolved from the award for faculty. Thank you, Mary Margaret McMahon Bullis, Marijo Rommelfaenger, and the ever-creative Katie Weis!

To the International Council of Nurses (ICN): Pam Cipriano, as then–first vice president, you introduced us to the organization that is the voice of the world's 28 million nurses. How proud we are that you are now ICN's global president. To Annette Kennedy: During your ICN presidency, you opened the doors wide for DAISY, providing a global showcase for our mission and even introducing us to the director-general of the World Health Organization, Dr. Tedros Adhanom Ghebreyesus. To Thomas Kearns: As interim CEO of ICN at the time of our introduction, you became a tremendous ambassador, bringing DAISY with you when you returned to your position as executive director of the Royal College of Surgeons-Ireland College of Nursing and Midwifery and the several hospitals with which it partners. And to Howard Catton and Michelle Acorn: Thank you for being gracious and welcoming leaders. We are so proud to know you both!

We also owe our thanks to numerous nursing organizations that support DAISY with mutual marketing efforts. Many of you honor your members and chapters with DAISY Health Equity Awards or DAISY Nurse Leader Awards. We are grateful to the leaders of each of these organizations for sharing our passion:

Academy of Forensic Nursing, Academy of Medical-Surgical Nurses, Alabama State Nurses Association, American Academy of Ambulatory Care Nursing, American Association for Men in Nursing, American Association of Nurse Practitioners, American Psychiatric Nurses Association, Arizona League of Nursing, Arkansas Association of Nurse Executives, Arkansas Nurses Association, Arkansas Organization of Nurse Executives, Army Nurse Corps Association, Asian American Pacific Islander Nurses Association, Association for Leadership Science in Nursing, Association for Nursing Professional Development, Association of California Nurse Leaders, Association of Pediatric Hematology/Oncology Nurses, Association of periOperative Nurses, Australian College of Neonatal Nurses;

Beryl Institute, Black Nurses Rock;

Canadian Association of Critical Care Nurses, Center for Nursing at the Foundation of NYS Nurses, CGFNS International, Chi Eta Phi Sorority, CNAI (Italian Nurses Association), Colorado Nurses Association, Competency & Credentialing Institute, Connecticut Center for Nursing Workforce;

Delaware Nurses Association, Delaware Organization for Nursing Leadership;

Emergency Nurses Association, Emirates Nursing Association, European Nursing Council;

Florence Nightingale Foundation;

The Arnold P. Gold Foundation;

HealthImpact, Hospice and Palliative Nurses Association;

Institute for Healthcare Improvement, Institute for Patient and Family-Centered Care, International Council of Nursing, International Home Care Nurses Organization, International Transplant Nurses Society, Irish Nurses and Midwives Organisation;

Maryland Organization of Nurse Leaders, Missouri Hospital Association, Missouri Organization of Nurse Leaders;

National Association of Directors of Nursing Administration, National Association of Hispanic Nurses, National Association of Indian Nurses of America, National Association of Travel Healthcare Organizations, National Black Nurses Association, National League for Nursing, National Organization of Nurses with Disabilities, Navy Nurse Corps Association, New Jersey League for Nursing, North Dakota Hospital Association, Nurse Practitioner Associates for Continuing Education, Nurses on Boards Coalition, Nursing Foundation of Pennsylvania, Nursing Institute of Healthcare Design;

Ohio League for Nursing, Oncology Nursing Society, Organization of Nurse Leaders;

Philippine Nurses Association of America, Planetree International;

The Schwartz Center for Compassionate Healthcare, Sepsis Alliance, Society of Head and Neck Nurses, Society of Internationally Educated Nurses, Society of Pediatric Nurses, Society of Trauma Nurses;

U-Vol Foundation;

Watson Caring Science Institute, World Federation of Neuroscience Nurses, Wound, Ostomy, and Continence Nurses Society.

❋ ❋ ❋

To the reviewers of the J. Patrick Barnes Grants for Nursing Research and Evidence-Based Practice Projects: You have spent untold hours carefully considering every submission, and we have learned so much listening in on your thoughtful deliberations about which work we should fund. Special heartfelt thanks to our panel chairs, Margaret Barton-Burke and Elizabeth Bridges: Your devotion to our mission to engage staff nurses in research demonstrates your focus on the future of nursing and healthcare. DAISY and all our applicants are the beneficiaries of the very generous time and brainpower contributed by Liz, Margaret, and Kelly Brassil, Gina Bufe, Jean Ann Connor, Laura Cullen, Kathleen Shannon Dorcy, Ann Dylis, Katherine Finn Davis, Anna Gawlinski, Elise Arsenault Knudsen, Mary Beth Flynn Makic, Kathy Oman, and Patricia Thomas. We could not do this without you. Thank you all!

To the reviewers of DAISY's Health Equity Grants: When we knew we had to do something to respond to George Floyd's murder and the immediate awareness of the inequities in our society, we launched our DAISY Health Equity Award and the DAISY Health Equity Grants. Thank you to the nurses who review applications of nurses doing research and EBP projects to address social determinants: Jennifer Baird, Carol Boswell, Andrea Carr, and Pat Span.

To Ann Hendrich and the Ann L. Hendrich Charitable Fund, in memory of Jim W. Hendrich: We were delighted when Ann, a nursing expert on older adults and former CNE at DAISY partner Ascension Health, reached out and urged us to include nurses who are working to improve the care and healthy aging of older adults in our health equity work. Thank you, Ann, for so generously underwriting these studies, and thank you Jennie Chin Hansen, Ying-Ling Jao, and Marvio Phillips for lending your brainpower and time to review these grant applications.

To the nurse-researchers: Your work has done so much: examining DAISY's impact on compassion fatigue and compassion satisfaction; analyzing DAISY nomination stories to add depth and insight into how patients and families describe extraordinary nurses; providing qualitative research to understand what it means to patients and families to say thank you to nurses by nominating them for a DAISY Award; connecting meaningful recognition to the elements of a healthy work environment and leadership styles. To Devin Bowers, Joanne Clavelle, Joyce Fitzpatrick, Melissa Foreman-Lovell, Susan Grant, Senem Guney, Lesly Kelly, Cindy Lefton, Rosanne Raso, Ellen Swartwout, Cindy Sweeney, and the many to come—thank you for your minds!

To the reviewers of DAISY's Medical Mission Grant applications: We felt strongly that we needed to support our DAISY Nurses who want to share their compassion and skill with people who live where quality healthcare is scarce. You help make this possible. Thank you Martha Abshire, Jose Arellano, Joanne Clavelle, Sally Lynne Easily, Joanne Evans, Jill Glenn, Stacy Kevener, Shellie Remenar, Andrea Segulin, Kelly Thompson, and Nia Wright.

To the reviewers of DAISY's Healing Hands Conference Grant program: As professional development budgets got smaller, you joined us to help DAISY Nurses achieve their continuing drive for knowledge. Thank you, Stephanie Al-Adhami, Cindy Angiulo, Will Carson, Regina Coll, Marvin Delvin, Signe Gilbert, Erin Glover, Mary Golway, Martha Grubaugh, Kimberly Knotts, Nancy Loos, Gewreka Nobles, Chris Schumacher, Jean Shinners, Wendy Silverstein, and the late Suzanne Taylor.

To the reviewers for the ANA DAISY Awards for Ethics in Practice and Leadership: The pandemic revealed to us the tremendous role ethics plays in patient care and nursing decision making, so we developed this national recognition in collaboration with the American Nurses Association's Center for Ethics and Human Rights. Stuart Downs, Nelda Godfrey, Cynda Rushton, and Liz Stokes worked tirelessly to create this program, which was presented for the first time at the 2024 National Nursing Ethics Conference. Thank you, Karen Grimley and UCLA Nursing for your generous sponsorship. In addition to Stuart, Nelda, and Cynda's discerning review of nominations, we are thankful to nursing ethicists Katherine Brown-Saltzman, Kara Curry, Margie Sip, and Carol Taylor for bringing your expertise to the tough task of choosing our inaugural honorees.

To the reviewers of the DAISY Awards for Extraordinary Nurses in Safety, in collaboration with the Institute for Healthcare Improvement: There is nothing more compassionate than saving a life, so we are very proud of this international award we have been giving out for over a decade. Thank you Cynthia Barginere, Christa Bedord-Mu, Hannah Cliatt, Shannon Conner Phillips, Ric Cuming, Ann Evans, Kathy Gorman, Helen Haskell, Ellen (Boo) Lahman, and Jeff Schultz. You make this happen!

To the reviewers of the HealthImpact DAISY Awards for Nurses in Policy: We often say that we had no business plan or real vision for The DAISY Foundation when we started it. We surely could never have imagined that we would be partnering with the brilliant and wonderful Garrett Chan and HealthImpact to honor nurses who advance compassionate care through policy. The reviewers who give their time and thinking to this award are Kit Bredimus, Carol Conroy, Raya Cupler, Timian Godfrey, Charley Larsen, Joan O'Hanlon Curry, and Deb Washington. Thank you all!

✿ ✿ ✿

To our Academic Research Collaborative (the schools of nursing at Chamberlain University, the University of Arizona, and University of South Florida): The gap in the literature on the impact of DAISY on nursing faculty needed to be filled, and you rose to fill it with a longitudinal study. Thank you Danika Bowen, Timian Godfrey, Karlene Kerfoot, Tonya Kimber Jones, Cheryl Lacasse, Loreal Newson, Susan Parda-Watters, Cindy Rishel, Deleise Wilson, and Ken Wofford.

To our International Ambassadors: Thank you Nancy Blake, Punjapon Boonchua, Susan Brown, Sandie Carlson, Racha Abou Chahine, Carolyn Fox, Sharon Jackson, Kerry Jones, Maricarmen Luhrsen, Mary Shepler and Madelyn Torakis for introducing us to new and mentoring new partners and serving as outstanding sounding boards and advisors.

❀ ❀ ❀

To our generous donors and supporters who helped us establish DAISY, especially in the early days: Matt Leible, Artie Marino, the late Tom Martin, Richard Schaps, David Yacullo, and Lamar Outdoor (Patrick's employer in Amarillo), you were Patrick's and our business colleagues in the advertising and billboard business and got us started with generous contributions in his memory—thank you! Bob and Yphon LaRoche (Tena and Pat's neighbors in Amarillo): You were so helpful when we started DAISY. Carolyn and Matt Wood: Thank you for never letting a Christmas go by without a generous donation to our mission. Bill Clark, Diane Frankel, Donna and Ed Horner, Patrick Lynch, Stacy and Dave Parks, and Charlie White: Thank you for keeping DAISY on your list of donations, always believing in what we do, and being so tolerant of all the times DAISY kept us from being around.

And one final thanks to the families of nurses who have died and who requested donations come to DAISY in lieu of flowers. To think that we meant so much to these nurses warms our hearts, and we are grateful to the countless people who have honored their lives by donating to us.

❀ ❀ ❀

To our Industry Partners: Thank you for sharing our passion for nurses and developing such mutually beneficial relationships.

To Cinnabon: Your delicious cinnamon rolls were part of DAISY celebrations for years and years. You donated more than 1 million cinnamon rolls to nurses! Jennifer Dempsey and Geoff Hill, our gratitude for creating our relationship is profound. To the many executives who sustained our relationship until DAISY just got too big, thank you! And thank you to the company's franchise partners, with a special salute to the creator of the world's best cinnamon roll, Jerilyn Brusseau.

To Get Well (Industry Partner since 2008): When CNO Connie Clemmons-Brown asked if she could accept DAISY Award nominations via your platform, we had never heard of your technology that helped patients become more engaged in their own care. So Connie introduced us. Mike Schram: You understood the value of our mission immediately and made it possible for patients in hospitals that used the technology to nominate their nurses through the system. You also introduced us to Michael O'Neil, who created the company out of his personal experience with healthcare as a young man with lymphoma who had no control over his own care and never wanted others to feel the same way. Michael: You served on our board and brought a great perspective and view of our future, not to mention a wonderful spirit, to every meeting and interaction. In addition, the warmth and support of every member of your team has made working with them a joy. Thank you to today's team supporting our partnership: Cliff Boeglin, Robin Cavenaugh, Bill Chatterton, Robin Forester, Holly Murphy, Joe Nora, Courtney Scott, Andy Selyutin, Jodi Smith, Jennifer Taylor, Katherine Virkstis, and Josh Young.

To Baxter (formerly Hill-Rom, an Industry Partner since 2008): Our relationship began thanks to the vision of Melissa Fitzpatrick, who worked for Hill-Rom at the time. Today our relationship with you has been enriched by the many people who have engaged with DAISY in the past and present, including Rummy Bajwa, Jason Bill, Kirsten Emmons, and James Teaff.

To Careismatic Brands (Industry Partner since 2010): Mike Singer, when you were CEO, you chose the DAISY Foundation as one of the ways to express the company's dedication to the nursing profession. Sponsoring DAISY Health Equity Awards for numerous organizations and Indian Health Service hospitals, the DAISY Breakfast for Pathway to Excellence for ANCC Conference attendees, producing our website's home page video that tells DAISY's story, and the magnificent video *Tribute to Nurses Courage*, shared globally during the pandemic, are just some of the tremendous contributions Careismatic makes to our mission. We are grateful for the many contributions of CBI's team over the years, including Michael Alexander, Micah Foster, Sid Lakhani, Paul McAdam, Kevin Mitchael, Haylee Newton, Torin Rea, Renata Ritcheson, Talal Sadeh, and Debbie Singer.

To symplr (Industry Partner since 2012, previously as API Healthcare): We cannot hope to recount all the ways you have collaborated with us since you acquired API. So we'll name just a few and the people behind them. Within minutes of the invitations going out, seats "sell out" to our annual DAISY Breakfast at the Magnet conference, which you have been sponsoring since 2014. BJ Schaknowski, your breakfast closing remarks each year are now legendary, and your support for DAISY's mission—not to mention the personal friendship we have developed—knows no bounds. Patti Dorgan and Karlene Kerfoot: The book of nurses' notes about DAISY you collected and gave us at the 2019 breakfast commemorating DAISY's 20th anniversary was a priceless gift; every note touched us deeply. The symplr exhibit hall booths at nursing conferences are graced with human-size daisies and splash our partnership throughout. You have taught us much about how companies can leverage their philanthropy to DAISY. Ann Joyal and Kristin Russel: It is so much fun when you travel with us to visit hospitals and celebrate nurses; your experience with DAISY Nurses led to the creation of three incredibly moving *Moments That Matter* video stories featuring DAISY Honorees. Finally, to everyone who elevates DAISY's visibility within symplr and externally: We are eternally grateful. Special thanks to Paul Billingsly, Lois Evans, Brian Fugere, Megan Hartman, Melissa Hoyos, Ali Morin, Amy Randolph, and Monica Tafoya. And one more huge thank-you to our dear friend and DAISY board member and DAISY Lifetime Achievement Award Honoree, Karlene Kerfoot.

To Chamberlain University (the country's largest school of nursing, DAISY's Foundation Educational Partner and Industry Partner since 2013): Peggy Guillory, you started what we know will be a lifelong friendship when you told us that you had gone to meet with CNO Stuart Downs and found his office filled with DAISY goodies for a DAISY Award presentation to one of his nurses. You called us shortly after the presentation to ask about sponsorship opportunities, and enlisted your colleague Ken Malito, knowing his engagement would really help ensure that a partnership would ensue. The result today is that every DAISY Honoree is entitled to a reduction in tuition at Chamberlain, and Chamberlain faculty and students are recognized with the DAISY Award in a robust and truly meaningful DAISY Award program. We took a deep breath of courage when we asked Chamberlain's President Karen Cox to join our board following her term as president of the American Academy of Nursing. Her commitment to compassion in nursing made her the perfect person to guide us in all things academic. Karen "gave us" Danika Bowen to partner with, who makes things happen at every level. We are so excited about the compassion courses you have developed and we are co-branding. Big thanks to all at Chamberlain who make a difference for DAISY: Kim Brandt, Anne Freichs, Susan Groenwald, Tonya Kimber-Jones, Beth Marguez, Jill Price, Carla Sanderson, and the army of workforce development specialists who travel with our staff to DAISY presentations and even attend on their own, a fresh bouquet of daisies at the ready for the honoree of the day.

To Kirby Bates Associates (KBA, Industry Partner since 2013): The late Karen Kirby was the first of our industry partners to put our DAISY Partner logo in her email signature, and she trooped around the country visiting hospitals with us. Our dear friend Melissa Fitzpatrick is now at the company's helm, and she has elevated our partnership to new heights. KBA sponsors the DAISY Breakfast at the AONL conference, and among the many things she does for DAISY, Lorrie Anderson makes sure the room is decked out to celebrate our partnership. Together, we mounted a webinar series for nurse leaders that we still talk about with pride. We thank Colleen Chapp, Jane Fitzsimmons, Jennifer Insua, Peggy Loughery, and KBA's parent company Jackson Health's Scott L'Heureux.

To Medtronic (Industry Partner since 2016): Patty Reilly, from the moment Ann Evans introduced us, you wanted to help, and navigated your way through the complex Medtronic system, with the help of Doug Bartlett whose devotion to nurses was tangible. It wasn't long before you instructed us on how to apply for a grant from Medtronic, and the company joined our roster of Industry Partners. Your team members are great traveling partners who love attending DAISY celebrations, so they stay connected to the real work of the people who use their devices and products—nurses. We love our shared reception for CNOs at the AONL conference, where we get to brag about how wonderful you all are. A huge thank-you to Brett Belokin, Alex Binczyk, Frank Chan, John Guarino, Caitlin Mayer, Jeff McIntosh, Michael Noble, Matt Regus, Brian Rosekrans, Robert St. John, Blake Tatum, and Linda Vang.

To CeraVe (Industry Partner since 2022): Who would have thought that DAISY would have a consumer skincare brand as an Industry Partner? But it's not just any skincare brand—it's the brand nurses love, not only because it is so wonderful for their skin but also because the company is a fierce advocate for nurses. We are beyond grateful to Tom Allison for welcoming us and the DAISY Coordinators of Manhattan to the company's headquarters for a terrific reception and inspiring presentation of Compassion Purpose Reimagined (CPR) by the remarkable Tena Brown and Andrea Coyle. Tena, your passion for nurses and energy to advocate for them could power all of your home state of Oklahoma. Thank you Caitlin King, for creating a beautiful Nurses Week video sharing the story of two DAISY Nurses and their patient and her baby—and then running it as an ad in *The New York Times*! Your conference exhibits are always jam-packed with nurses lining up to get the products they love, and now they see our partnership beautifully decorating your booth. Our plan to join forces in advocating for nurses is building momentum, and we are very excited to see the impact on nurses. Thank you Tom, Scott Carpenter, Jasteena Gill, Helen Lynch, Kerri Petrakis, and the entire team.

To Press Ganey (Industry Partner since 2022): For years we hoped to partner with you to help bring DAISY recognition to many more nurses by making patients aware of the opportunity to nominate their nurses via your surveys. To Mary Jo Assi, Jeff Doucette, Nicole George, Pat Ryan, and Nora Warshawsky: Thank you for bringing this dream to life. It is working! Your partnership is invaluable.

To Prolucent (Industry Partner since 2022): Jeff Ondeck, you saw the potential for making DAISY a filter in your Liquid Compass job search engine. Carol Bradley and Kathy Douglas, your decades-long commitment to DAISY in various roles before you joined Prolucent brought us back together when you joined forces with Bruce Springer and Derek Quackenbush. Now we are delighted that Pat Gundersen has joined your team, and look forward to what we will do together. Thank you for your continued support and understanding of what makes DAISY meaningful recognition.

To Qualtrics (Industry Partner since 2022): When Adrienne Boissy reached out to offer the company's support, we were blown away. Her reputation as a physician and patient experience expert preceded her. What we did not know was that she had been working for years on how to lend support to our mission of gratitude to nurses. We could not have envisioned how much Qualtrics's support would come to mean as we turn to your technology to support DAISY's infrastructure, see how you are working to make DAISY easier for our coordinators in their client health systems, and encourage more nominations through your surveys. Thank you, Nick Apeland, Bryanna Galloway, Geraldine Lim, Levi Nation, Zig Serafin, Brian Stucki, and Denise Venditti.

To Propelus (Industry Partner since 2023): We were saddened when Julie Walker left symplr to become CEO of Propelus. The daughter of a nurse, Julie has a huge soft spot in her heart for the profession. But Julie promised to support DAISY at Propelus—and within months we were partners. Thank you, Julie, John Barnes, Jessica Dunbar, Karen Griffin, Alex Lauderdale, Justin Mann, Kelly Parker, Joshua Scott, and Lindsey Stickney. We are proud of all your support and the opportunity to introduce the brand to our DAISY community.

To SE Healthcare (Industry Partner since 2024): Our long-time friendship with Andrea Coyle, who was our DAISY coordinator at the Medical University of South Carolina for years, has blossomed into partnership with both CeraVe and now SE Healthcare. The company's

Nurse Burnout Prevention platform is making a difference for nurses, and we are thrilled that CEO Greg Cottichia saw the value in partnering with DAISY as soon as he joined the company.

To our International Advocate, Health Carousel: Your approach to nurse recruiting and holding up the highest of ethics in the field is beautifully aligned with DAISY's values. Today, the Health Carousel Foundation supports our program in Cameroon, Ghana, Liberia, the Philippines, and Uganda. We know you will continue to drive our international reach and make it possible for organizations that could never afford to recognize their nurses do so. We are so proud of our association with you: Nyra Colinares, Christy Craft, Earl Dalton, Connie dela Cruz, Michelle Hehman, Kyle Kenzie, Andrew Lingo, Donita Ross, Erik Schumann, and John Sebastian.

Finally, thank you to Nanne Finis and Martie Moore, special nurse friends who have worked hard to introduce us to potential industry partners.

❀ ❀ ❀

To the companies and people who help ensure that we serve our DAISY community well:

Greg Loveland of Crown Trophy in Petaluma, CA: Our hospital partners appreciate the plaques and pins you produce for us.

Kevin Jones and Shawn Morris of FastSigns of Santa Rosa: You produce our banners and signs so beautifully, and your service is truly excellent.

Renowned jewelry designer Ann Hand: Our board member Kathy Gorman introduced us to you when we launched the DAISY Lifetime Achievement Award. When we met with you and you heard our story, you offered to donate a specially designed pin for these extraordinary honorees.

Ryan's Custom Crating: Your crates help make sure the large Healer's Touch sculptures our partners place in healing gardens and lobbies arrive in one piece.

Joanie Schwartz: Your exquisite individually made fused glass daisy creations are treasured by our board, staff, and International DAISY

Day speakers. We know you never want to look at another daisy again, having hand-made hundreds of them for us.

Joe Tye: We believe that you now know more about DAISY than we do! The work you and your University of Iowa grad students did to build your case study was astounding. The resulting book, *How the DAISY Foundation Has Influenced the Global Healthcare Landscape*, takes our breath away—as does your generosity in donating it to so many nurses. We so appreciate Sally's and your underwriting DAISY programs in Guyana, and thank you for the two enormous pens you sent to get us started on this book, too. You are a true friend to us, the DAISY community, and the nursing profession.

Dennis Vaughan: You have been supplying our handsome DAISY Award certificate portfolios almost from the beginning of DAISY. They are a thousand percent improvement over the frames we were buying at Costco. (Nothing against Costco, of course.)

Wax Creative Medicine: Taking DAISY under the wing of your amazing marketing agency has been incredibly helpful. Thank you for all your creativity, support, and guidance as we build our social media presence, and for helping our website be even more effective. Your billboard designs during the pandemic helped us take advantage of over $1 million worth of donated billboard space urging the public to say thank you to their nurses by nominating them for the DAISY Award. Thank you, Craig Fairfield, Amanda Herriman, Rebecca Larger, and Bill Wax.

Phil Buck: You have been with us almost from the beginning, designing DAISY logos and collateral material. Thank you for always being there for us!

Nurse.com: Thank you for being a great supporter of DAISY's mission. Heather Cygan, Sallie Jimenez, and Cara Lumsford: We love sharing a blog with your readers each quarter, and so appreciate your amplifying DAISY news to your audience.

As we endeavor to ensure easy access for patients and families to nominate their nurses, it is a priority that we offer electronic means of submitting and tracking nomination. We are grateful to Get Well/Rounds+, nDorse (thank you Rohan Walvekar and Bryan Phou, for creating a beautiful platform for DAISY digital nominations!), HCI, Laudio, pcare, SONIFIhealth, TELEHEALTH Services, and 4U Medical Grade IV Bag Stickers.

❊ ❊ ❊

To our newest collaborator in nominations, AARP: It has long been our vision to engage with the public, encouraging more patients and families to express their gratitude to nurses by nominating them for DAISY Awards. Nurses can never have enough nominations! Imagine our joy when our friend Karen Drenkard, chief nursing advisor at the AARP Public Policy Institute, proposed we join forces with AARP for outreach to its members, urging them to express their gratitude to nurses! We have long admired AARP's initiatives in healthcare—and we have long been AARP members. To see DAISY Honorees featured in AARP media and ads, and to provide easy access to DAISY nomination forms for members is a dream come true! We launched the collaboration at the AONL conference in 2024, and we can't wait to see the impact. A huge thank-you to Karen and to Sarah Lovenheim, Jennifer Peed, Winifred Quinn, Susan Reinhard, Sarah Sonies, Ana Whitelock, and Ilse Zuniga for sharing our passion for nursing and understanding the importance of meaningfully recognizing nurses for all they do for the "rest of us."

❊ ❊ ❊

Who have we left out?

We have so many personal friends who stand by us as we dedicate our lives to DAISY, knowing we are often not home or available for social activities. But you are always interested in what we are doing for nurses and caring that we are healthy and happy. Lauri and Tim Dorman, Angie and Nick Frey, Val and the late Jerry Gibbons, Joan and the late Jim Griffin, Bonnie Lasky and Irv Rothenberg, Jamie and TeeJay Lowe, Vicki and Paul Michalcyzk, Andy and Krista Parker, Anna and Frank Pope, Chris and Jeff Prime, Joanie and Jim Schwartz, Gerry Simpson, Joanne and David Wilshin, and Sandy Zuckerman and her wonderful late husband Ira (who was with us for our first "aggressive discussion").

Thank you for being so wonderful and understanding, all of you.

❋ ❋ ❋

And last here but always first in our hearts: the nurses who have embraced, enhanced, and even built DAISY by telling each other about it and taking it from one organization to another.

To the hundreds of thousands of nurses who have been honored with the DAISY Award: We hope we helped you understand that by "just doing your job" you made a lasting impression on your patients.

To the millions of nurses who have been nominated: Please treasure the fact that people took the time to share stories of their care with you.

To the tens of thousands of DAISY coordinators, committee members, and administrative assistants: The DAISY Award comes to life with your dedication of time, creativity, resourcefulness, and passion for our mission.

To every CNO and CNE (the whole C-suite, for that matter) who understands, values, and supports meaningful recognition of nurses: You have shone the light on all the right.

You all have our undying gratitude. This story is yours as much as it is ours. We just want to say thank you, one more time. To all of you.

And to Our Patrick.

Index

Pages in *italics* are photographs
or illustrations. For names
not listed and for more cita-
tions of listed names, see
pages 203–227

A

AARP, 199, 226
Adventist Feather River
Hospital, 124
Al Amro, Abdullah, 104–105
Allen, Alicia, 191
Alta Bates Hospital, 44
America West Airlines, 41, 42
American Academy of Nursing,
151, 152
American Association for
Nursing Development, 89
American Association of
Colleges of Nursing (AACN),
128, 193

American Association of
Critical-Care Nurses (AACN),
64, 134–135, 141, 151
American Nurses Credentialing
Center (ANCC), 34, 100–101,
102, 107, 142, 151, *151*, 188, *188*
American Organization for
Nursing Leadership (AONL),
88, 93, 151, 171, 188, 197–198.
See also American Organization
of Nurse Executives
American Organization of
Nurse Executives (AONE),
46, 64, 88–93, 102, 111, 122,
135, 136, 141
American University Medical
Center (Beirut), 102
ANA DAISY Awards for Ethics
in Practice and Leadership,
195, 196, 217

Angiulo, Cindy, 29, 30, 32, 88, 120
Antoku, Marion, 62, 63
Ascher, Erin, 164, 165, 166, 193
"Auntie Bonkers." See Barnes, Melissa

B

Bacon, Angela, 25
Baptist Saint Anthony Medical Center, 4, 8, 39
Barnes, Adam, 8, 113
Barnes, Bonnie and Mark, *32, 103, 106, 115, 151, 188*
 inseparability, 152, 156
Barnes, Brad, 8
Barnes, Dianne, 8, 14, 20, 26, 29–30, 31, 41, 87, 120, 135
Barnes, J. Patrick, *15, 79*
 early life, 4, 6, 121
 illness with ITP, 3–5, 7–14
 nurses' care for, 7–8, 9, 10–11, 21–22, 150, 156
 "Our Patrick," 5, 6, 7, 13, 20, 83, 92, 107, 115, 150, 157
 positive character, 6, 7, 9, 11, 14, 21, 27, 28, 78, 79, 80
Barnes, Melissa, 107, 113–114, 115, *115,* 172–173, 177–178, 179, 184, 185, *188*
Barnes Carraher, Riley, 3–4, 6, 9, 11, 12, 14, *15,* 20, 26, 75, 78, *79, 106,* 109, 110, 113
Barnes Carraher, Tena, 3, 4–6, 7, 9, 10, 11–14, 21, 26, 75, 87, 109–111, 112, 114, 115, *115,* 120, 175, 176, 184, 185, *188*
 naming DAISY, 20, 22
 nurses' consideration for, 11–12, 21–22
Barton, Noah, 169
Behrendt, Rachel, 123, 124
"Beyond Gratitude: A Tribute to Nurse Managers," 198
Bierer, Leah R., 47–48
Bridges, Elizabeth, 121

Bronson Methodist Hospital, 154
Brown, Susan, 174
Brown, Gillian, 179
Buerhaus, Peter I., 196, 198–199
Bumrungrad International Hospital (Bangkok), 105

C

"Campaign for Nursing's Future," 196–197
Caramanica, Laura, 135, 136
Careismatic Brands, 175, 198
Carraher, John, 110
Carraher, Riley Barnes. See Barnes Carraher, Riley
Carraher, Tena. See Barnes Carraher, Tena
Cedars-Sinai Medical Center, 39, 82
Cesaretti, Leah M., 47–48
Chamberlain University, 128, 142, 199
Children's Hospital Cincinnati, *73*
Children's Hospital Los Angeles, 60–61, 62, 63, 64, 65, 78, 125
Children's Hospital Oakland, 44
Children's Hospital of Philadelphia, 179
Cinnabon, 7, 8, 28, 29, 42–43, 50, 52, 100, 110, 123
Coffman, Lisa, 62, 63
Cooper, Emily J., 67–70
COVID-19
 consequences for DAISY, 171–178, 179–180, 184
 consequences for nursing profession, 180, 193, 197
Crome, Patti, 88
Crow, Greg, 105–106

D

D'Aquila, Richard, 40
DAISY Award, 130. *See also specific awards*
 banner, DAISY, 72, *73,* 81, 91, 93, 105, 120

banner, "United in Caring," *172*, *173*, 174

certificate, 23, 28, 31, 50, 52, 76, 93, 114, 119

criteria for, 31, 32, 72, 80. *See also* nomination process

consequences of COVID-19 for, 171–178, 179–180

electronic billboards promoting, 176–177, *177*

first presentation, 31–32, *32*

gifts, 23, 27, 28, 29, 30, 31, 37, 38, 43, 45, 46, 49–50, 52, 61, 72, 74, 76, 112, 119, 120, 130. *See also* Cinnabon; *Healer's Touch* sculpture; pin

growth of, 34, 38–40, 61, 63, 64–67, 80, 81, 82, 93, 100, 102, 107, 111, 112–113, 150–151, 180, 195

impact on nurses, 25, 37, 45, 49, 59, 71, 74, 75–76, 78, 87, 99, 119, 122, 127, 130, 133, 138–142, 149, 155, 187–188, 191–199

impact on organizations, 33, 44, 45, 61, 63, 65–66, 74, 75, 80–81, 89–90, 93, 107, 109, 112, 125, 126, 138–142, 193–194

initial ideas for, 21–23, 27–28, 29–30

internationalism, 100–107, 180

limits on, 125–126

nomination process, 29, 31, 32, 33, 46, 63, 66, 72, 74, 75–76, 80, 81, 105, 114, 176, 177–178

nurses' acceptance of concept, 28, 32, 75, 78–79

nurses' expansion of concept, 72–74, 78–79, 119–130, 152, *153*, *175*

QR code for nominations, 176, 178

pin, 23, 28, 37, 50, 52, 72, 74, 112, 120, 130, 185, 192–193, *192*

reach of, 130, 150

research on impact of, 134–142, 170–171, 174

scrapbooks, 78, 79, 165

as tool for nurse retention and recruitment, 193–194

"United in Caring" campaign, *172*, 173–174, *173*

DAISY Award for Advancing Health Equity, 195–196, 213, 215

DAISY Award for Ethics in Practice and Leadership, 195, 196

DAISY Award for Extraordinary Nurse Educators, 180, 212, 213. *See also* DAISY Faculty Award

DAISY Award for Extraordinary Nurses in Patient Safety, 213, 217

DAISY Award for Extraordinary Nursing Students, 129

DAISY Award for Nurse-Led Teams. *See* DAISY Team Award

DAISY Award for Nurses in Policy, 196, 217

DAISY Champion recognition, 126–127

"DAISY Dust," 43

DAISY Faculty Award, 65, 127–129, 142

DAISY Foundation
   awards and recognition for, 106, 144, 151, 151–152, 167
   board members, 43, 44, 63, 64, 65, 67, 87–88, 110, 115, 116, 120, 121, 125, 127, 150, 167. *See also* *individual names*
   collaborations, 196, 198, 217
   consequences of COVID-19 for, 171–178, 179–180, 184
   corporate sponsors, 41, 42, 64, 81, 82. *See also specific companies*
   database, 67, 83, 91
   funding by, 27, 120–121
   funding of, 23, 26, 41, 64, 80, 81–83, 87–88, 91, 92–93

future of, 186, 189
initial ideas for, 20, 22–23, 26–27, 45
naming, 20
newsletter, 41, 78, 79
operations, 55, 67, 111, 112, 113–116, 136, 164
research grants, 120–121, 175
website, 24, 41, 44, 72, 78, 114, 176, 185
DAISY Founders' Coin, 126
DAISY Health Equity Grants, 215
DAISY Lifetime Achievement Award, 129, 130
DAISY Medical Mission Grants, 121
DAISY Model of Impact, 142–143, *143*
DAISY Nurse Leader Award, 122, 127, 180, 198
DAISY Team Award, 119, 122, *123*, 123–125, 126, 127, 130, 180
Dan (nurse in Amarillo), 7, 21
Dechairo-Marino, Ann, 45, 46, 61
Dempsey, Jennifer, 43
Dexter, Madeline, 190
Doll, Lynne, 39, 82, 121
Duerksen, Christine, 99

E
Edwards, Debbie Zahren, 59
England, Judy and Bruce, 39
Evans, Ann, 63–64, 66, 88

F
Fiddler, John, 40–41
Fitzpatrick, Melissa, 42
Floyd, Jeanne, 100–101
Foreman-Lovell, Melissa, 142, 170
Fred Hutchinson Cancer Research Center, 8, 9, 14, 20, 21, 28, 29, 30–31

G
George, James, 8, 26
Gergely, Sue, 90, 91
Godfrey, Cynthia, 40
Grady Memorial Hospital, 154

Grant, Susan, 29, 33–34, 65, 66, 75, 142, 170
Griffey, 8, 14
Griffin, Joan and Jim, 164
Groenwald, Susan, 128, 142
Gull, Gill, 108

H
Hacker, Mary Dee, 60–62, 63, 64–65, 66, 78, 88, 125
Hartzog, Meredith, 119
Healer's Touch sculpture, 46, 49–52, *51*, *54*, 55–56, 119, 129, 130, 165–166, *166*, 167, *172*, 173, 174. *See also* Mother and Child
Health Alliance of Greater Cincinnati, 65
HealthImpact DAISY Awards for Nurses in Policy, 196, 217
Heyman, Beth, 65, 66, 88, 127
Hill, Geoff, 43
Hilliard, Donna, 102, 103, 104
Hill-Rom, 42
Hospice of the Valley, 41, 42
Hospital for Sick Children (Toronto), 102
Hospital of the University of Pennsylvania, 179
Hospital Israelita Albert Einstein (São Paulo), 105
Hurn, Patty, 127, 128

I
Idiopathic thrombocytopenic purpura. *See* ITP
Impact Model, DAISY, 142–143, *143*
In the Year of the Nurse—A Tribute to Courage, 175, 198
Intensive Care Unit Team, Southern New Hampshire Medical Center ICU, 35–36
International Council of Nursing, 107
ITP, 3–5, 7–8, 10, 13, 150
Support Association (UK), 27

supporting research to treat and cure, 20, 23, 26–27, 78, 79, 120, 121

J

J. Patrick Barnes Grants for Nursing Research and Evidence-Based Practice Projects, 120–121

Jackson, Quinn C., 117

Jairamani, Christina, 185

Johnson & Johnson, 41, 196

Johnson, Rebecca, 71

Joslin, Daryl, 197

Jutte, Paul, *192*

K

Kamstra, Jane, 88

Karen (nurse in Seattle), 12–13, 21

Kearns, Thomas, 144

Kelly, Lesly, 141–142

King Fahad Medical City, 102, 104–105

King Faisal Specialist Hospital and Research Centre, 100, 101, 102, *103*

Koloroutis, Mary, 143

L

Lasky, Bonnie, 43–44, 60, 88

Lefton, Cindy, 135–141, 142, 144, 187, 194

Levine, Susan Goldwater, 41–42

Lovering, Sandy and Craig, 100

Lower Keys Medical Center, *154*

Lynch, Rob, 178

Lynne Doll Grants for Dissemination of Findings, 121

M

Magill, Jennifer, 19

Magnet Recognition Program®, 34, 65–66, 80–81, 100–101, 102, 116, *116*, 141, 142, 151, *151*, 187, 188, *188*

Maher, Peter, *106*, 115–116, 184

McClellan, Laura, 142

Meadows, MT, 90, 91

Memorial Sloan Kettering Cancer Center, 78

Mercy San Juan Medical Center, 78, *79*

Morton Plant Mease Health Care, *153*

Mohammad, Amal Awni, 131–132

Moseley, Judy, 101–102

Mother and Child sculpture, 50–52, 53, 54

Mowatt, Megan, 37

Muro, Nicolette, 84–85

N

National Council of State Boards of Nursing (NCSBN), 193

NewYork-Presbyterian Weill Cornell Medical Center, 40

Northampton General Hospital (England), 105

Northridge Medical Center, 45

Nottingham University Hospitals NHS Trust, 105, *106*

Nurse recognition program. *See* DAISY Award

O

Oncology Team Snow Day, UCLA Medical Center Santa Monica, 56–58

Opseth, Greg, 87

Organization of Associate Degree Nurses, 128

OSF Saint Francis Medical Center, 74

Our Lady of Lourdes (Drogheda, Ireland), 178–179

P

Pakieser-Reed, Katherine, 149

Piedmont Hospital, 110, 111

Platelet Disorder Support Association, 27

Providence St. Vincent's Hospital, 72, *73*

R

Renown Health. *See* Washoe Medical Center

Reynolds, John, 53–56, 67, 111

Rice, Janet, 129

Riley Children's Hospital, 110
Robert (nurse in Amarillo), 9
Robinson, Carol, 44
Robison, Michele, 49
Royal College of Surgeons School of
    Nursing and Midwifery (Dublin),
    144, 179
Runnels, Wesley, 94–95

S

SalesForce, 91, 113, 114
San Francisco General Hospital, 44,
    78, 106
Sanchez, Cindy J. Ovalle, 168
Sanchez, Lauren, 158–159
Santa Rosa Memorial Hospital, 39, 52
Saudi Arabia, 99–105, 107
Schafer, Monica, 183
Schmit, Rebecca, 23–24
Schoen, Alex, 150, 185
Scott, Rhonda, 154
Seattle Cancer Care Alliance, 28, 29–33,
    34
Shangrove, Kenna Smith, 31–32, *32*
Sigma Theta Tau International Honor
    Society of Nursing, 107, 151
Silvestri, Janet, 178, 185
Sipe, Margie, 133
Sonoma Valley Hospital, 39, 52
Staniecki, Anna, 145–148
Stewart, Deidre, 102
Stormer, Carolyn, 31–32
Suga, Melanie, 145–148
Surgical Care Unit at Children's
    National Medical Center, *123*
Swaim, Jane, 71–72
Sweeney, Cindy, 142–143, 170–171, 185
symplr, 198

T

Tana (nurse in Seattle), 12, 21, 133, 134
Thomas Jefferson University Methodist
    Hospital, 123, *153*
Thompson, Pam, 88, 89–93
Tisdale, Lori, 181
Trautman, Deb, 128
Turme, Steve, 39

U

"United in Caring, Courage and
    Compassion," *172*, 173–174, *173*
UnitedHealthcare, 82
University of Iowa Hospitals and
    Clinics, 129
University of Washington (UW)
    Medical Center, 28–33, 34, 38, 39,
    65, 88, 110, 120
USAir. *See* America West

V

Vogus, Timothy, 142

W

Wain, Bea, 59–60
Washoe Medical Center, 39
Weedman, Jonathan, 64
Wells Fargo Foundation, 64
Westchester Medical Center, 135, 136
Wilshaw, Jane, 104
Wojnar, Christopher, 163

Y

Young, Donna, 109

Z

Zimmermann, Deb, 186–189, *188*